TOMORROW
and
TOMORROW
and
TOMORROW

TOMORROW
and
TOMORROW
and
TOMORROW

Edited by
David G. Yellin and Marie Connors

With a Foreword by Judith Crist

UNIVERSITY PRESS OF MISSISSIPPI
JACKSON

Library of Congress Cataloging in Publication Data

Main entry under title:
Tomorrow and Tomorrow and Tomorrow,

   Bibliography: p.
   "Faulkner, a television and film checklist": p.
   Contents: The short story "Tomorrow" / by William
Faulkner—The television play "Tomorrow" / by Horton
Foote—The film: *Tomorrow* by Horton Foote. The price of
independence / by Gilbert Pearlman and Paul Roebling.
You must draw from within yourself / by Robert Duvall.
On playing Sarah / by Olga Bellin. Directing: to
reveal the behavior of people / by Joseph Anthony.
Editing a love one / by Reva Schlesinger.
   1. Tomorrow (Motion picture)—Addresses, essays,
lectures.   2. Foote, Horton. Tomorrow—Addresses,
essays, lectures.   3. Faulkner, William, 1897–1962.
Tomorrow—Addresses, essays, lectures.   4. Faulkner,
William, 1897–1962—Film adaptations—Addresses, essays
lectures.   I. Yellin, David G.   II. Connors, Marie.
III. Faulkner, William, 1897–1962. Tomorrow.   1985.
IV. Foote, Horton. Tomorrow.   1985.   V. Tomorrow
(Motion picture)
PN1997.T5963T6   1985   791.43′72   84-21908
ISBN 0-87805-247-X
ISBN 0-87805-248-8 (pbk.)

CONTENTS

ACKNOWLEDGMENTS

THE EDITORS wish to thank the numerous persons who assisted us in our journey through "Tomorrow" and "Tomorrow" and *Tomorrow*. The members of David Yellin's Comparative Media Seminar at Memphis State University provided helpful insights and indeed the inspiration for this book. We couldn't have done this book without the interviews on the phone and in person with Horton Foote, Gilbert Pearlman, Paul Roebling, Robert Duvall, Olga Bellin, Joseph Anthony and Reva Schlesinger. We are grateful to Mr. and Mrs. Richard L. Lightman who graciously permitted our graduate seminar to view the film version of *Tomorrow* in their private theatre. Two Memphis State University English professors contributed significantly to our understanding of the literary aspects of comparative media. Dr. Helen White presented an informative essay on the short story form and Dr. James Newcomb delivered an excellent lecture in which he skillfully analyzed Faulkner's story. Some of their remarks have been incorporated into the introduction. We want to express our gratitude to Lawrence Wells, publisher of Yoknapatawpha Press, for his faith and encouragement. Our sincere appreciation also extends to those who helped us complete the manuscript including: Dr. Patricia E. Connors, English Department, and Jane Qualls and Sharon Tucker of the Brister Library, Memphis State University; Tom Welsh of Yale University; Jane Isbell Haynes of Memphis; typists Sharon Chesher and Dee Fonville; and photographer John Lynch. Our final, most heartfelt thanks goes to Carol Lynn Yellin for her generous and expert editorial advice.

Grateful acknowledgment is made to the following for permission to reprint copyrighted material used in this book:

"Tomorrow"
Copyright 1940 and renewed 1968 by Estelle Faulkner and Jill Faulkner Summers. Copyright 1949 by William Faulkner. Reprinted from *Knight's Gambit*, by William Faulkner, by permission of Random House, Inc.

Excerpts from *"Tomorrow:* The Genesis of a Screenplay" and "On First Dramatizing Faulkner" by Horton Foote.

Reprinted from *Faulkner, Modernism, and Film,* edited by Evans Harrington and Ann J. Abadie, by permission of The University of Mississippi and The University Press of Mississippi. Copyright © 1979 by The University Press of Mississippi.

The photographs used in this book are printed courtesy of *The Saturday Evening Post* (part I), Columbia Broadcasting System (part II), and Filmgroup Productions (part III).

Facts about the CBS production of "Tomorrow" included in the introductory essay are from the Brodkin Archive, collection of American Literature, the Beinecke Rare Book and Manuscript Library, Yale University.

This work was supported in part by a grant from Memphis State University Faculty Research Grant Fund. This support does not necessarily imply endorsement of research conclusions by the university.

FOREWORD

THERE ARE SPECIAL beloveds in a critic's life that go beyond the biggies, the neoclassics, and the instant "masterpieces" we discover on a daily, weekly, or monthly basis. The special beloveds are the unexpected films, the "sleepers" that arrive without fanfare, are viewed without expectations, and make an indelible mark on memory and heart. *Tomorrow* is such a film.

I fell in love with *Tomorrow* in April of 1972 and it wound up on my "Ten Best" list along with such equally memorable but far more popularly acclaimed films as *Cries and Whispers, The Sorrow and the Pity, The Discreet Charm of the Bourgeoisie, Slaughterhouse-Five, Cabaret, Sleuth, Sounder, The Emigrants,* and another special film, *Images.* Through the years I have spread the gospel of *Tomorrow,* offering it in "critic's choice" series, urging it on college film society programs, using it as a lecture supplement, showing it again—and again—at the Tarrytown Conference Center film weekends I've been conducting for fourteen years.

Why the passion for the film *Tomorrow?* It stems primarily from its being the first, and probably the only film to re-create the world of William Faulkner in both the letter and the spirit of his masterful creations. A primitive black-and-white movie made in Faulkner's Frenchman's Bend area of Mississippi, *Tomorrow* tells of a love and a commitment between inarticulate persons who cannot allow themselves the comprehension of love or afford a choice between pursuing it and "keepin' on breathin'," but who sustain with inner passion the burdens of existence. On film, with the camera providing the actuality of the lives observed and Robert Duvall and Olga Bellin creating those lives with a profoundly moving insight, the story comes to life as a paean to the steadfastness, the endurance, and the nobility of "the lowly" of whom Faulkner immortalized with love.

One says "the story" and therein lies the source of the film and the fascinating study that awaits you in this book. The film is rooted, in fact, in a short story published in *The Saturday Evening Post* in 1940 and reprinted in 1949 in *Knight's Gambit*. Twenty years after it was first published, Horton Foote derived a teleplay from it for CBS's Playhouse 90, and twelve years later he provided a screenplay to be directed by Joseph Anthony. That the film is suggestive of the stage in its drama of characters is not surprising, given its subject and the background of its creators.

I used the term "study" in referring to the comparison of media that this volume provides. I think "adventure" is a better word for the experience David Yellin has been providing through his comparative media courses at Memphis State University and that he and Marie Connors offer in this book. What better adventure than to trace the creative process within the strictures of a variety of media? How better to understand each medium, its confines and its possibilities, than by tracing the transition of a novel to a stageplay to a television drama to a film. One can also consider such classic adaptations as *The Caine Mutiny* or *Romeo and Juliet* as it moves from the theater to ballet to three film versions. I think a comparison of Peter Benchley's novel *Jaws* with Steven Spielberg's film is a classic example of what constitutes good fiction and exactly which of the elements of fiction satisfy the demands of cinema. Beyond the comparison of manuscripts, scenarios, teleplays, and librettos there are the considerations of the audience and of the experiences of reading and of viewing. You can examine these and many other factors as Faulkner's "Tomorrow" goes from short story to teleplay to film.

Since feature films began, their roots have been in fiction, in biography, and in stageplays. Nowadays original films even spawn their own book and television versions. Forth and back we go in our multimedia days. But rare indeed is the fidelity to the original creator's intent that you will find in the two Horton Foote dramatizations of Faulkner's story. And beyond the fidelity, this comparative media adventure allows you to share with the various collaborators of the film their experiences—from inspiring to frustrating—creating in cinematic form what Yellin and Connors have termed "a heightening of the work's integrity and a strengthening of its dynamics."

Enjoy the adventure. And I hope you will join us in our passion for "Tomorrow" and "Tomorrow" and *Tomorrow*.

Judith Crist

TOMORROW
and
TOMORROW
and
TOMORROW

FAULKNER AND FOOTE AND CHEMISTRY

David Yellin and Marie Connors

THIS BOOK is about the evolution of a classic film which grew out of a highly rated television drama adapted from a short story by William Faulkner. Faulkner's original story was published in the *Saturday Evening Post* of 23 November 1940. Horton Foote's television play was first aired live on the CBS-TV network's Playhouse 90 on 7 March 1960, and repeated on tape 18 July 1961. Foote's film version was released 9 April 1972. In recounting these transformations of "Tomorrow" and in analyzing the creative chemistry that made them work, our emphasis is on understanding the three media: their characteristics and techniques, where and how they differ, and what happens to a work when it is transported into another form. We compare "Tomorrow" and "Tomorrow" and *Tomorrow* in order to better appreciate not only the distinctive qualities of all three media but also the unique creative contributions of William Faulkner and Horton Foote and his collaborators.

We have a solid base from which to make our comparisons. Each of the three versions of "Tomorrow" sets out to tell a story and each pursues the same mystery: why juryman Jackson Fentry can't vote Bookwright free for killing Buck Thorpe. Also, in restructuring the form and plot of the Faulkner story, Horton Foote retains in each visual version the theme of the original tale—the hope that tomorrow symbolizes for "the lowly and invincible of the earth," to use the words that Faulkner gives to the lawyer Gavin Stevens. It is a theme that reminds us of lines from his 1950 Nobel Prize acceptance speech:

> I believe that man will not merely endure: he will prevail. He is immortal, not because he alone among creatures has an inexhaustible voice, but because he has a soul, a spirit capable of compassion and sacrifice and endurance. The poet's, the writer's, duty is to write about these things. It is his privilege to help man endure by lifting his heart, by reminding him of the courage and honor and hope and pride and compassion and pity and sacrifice which have been the glory of his past. The poet's voice need not be the record of man, it can be one of the props, the pillars to help him endure and prevail.

3

With this as a frame of reference, we are ready to make our journey into the short story "Tomorrow," the live television drama "Tomorrow," and the film *Tomorrow*, looking at each in order of creation and observing how the dramatizations can heighten the work's integrity and strengthen its dynamics.

THE SHORT STORY

Not long before William Faulkner sold "Tomorrow" to the *Saturday Evening Post* for a thousand dollars in 1940, he wrote his publisher that he was "still writing short stories" and that some of them were "bound to sell" soon. "If I can sell one for top price, it will get me through to October, which will give me two months to write and sell another."[1] In another letter written the same year he says that he has been "trying to write the sort of pot boilers which the Post pays me $1,000.00 each for," and adds that "the best I could hope for good stories is 3 or 4 hundred."[2]

The American magazine had long been the mass medium through which the short story flourished. Since the early nineteenth century it had offered a welcome and sometimes lucrative market-place for many a hard-pressed writer, including such diverse talents as Edgar Allan Poe, Nathaniel Hawthorne, O. Henry, Sherwood Anderson, and—in more recent times—Ernest Hemingway, F. Scott Fitzgerald, and William Faulkner. But magazine editors in Faulkner's day, particularly editors of such slick-paper publications as the *Post* and *Collier's* attempted to reach the "composite reader," and in doing so frequently published "formula fiction" dismissed by critics as having no lasting literary value. One of the most popular genres was the mystery story and "Tomorrow" roughly fits into this category.

Faulkner, like others before him, wrote stories for the magazines for the money. At various intervals in the 1930s and early 1940s he also sojourned to Hollywood as a screenwriter for the same reason—to make enough money to sustain himself so that he could write his novels, the source of his reputation. Evidence exists, however, that he gave more than passing consideration to this story of Stonewall Jackson Fentry and why he stood firm against the others on the jury. In 1942, two years after the story was published in the *Post*, Faulkner considered turning "Tomorrow" into a screenplay. Seven years later he included it in *Knight's Gambit*, a loosely connected collection of his short stories that has been largely ignored by both the public and the critics.

Regardless of the neglect the story has suffered because of its association with Faulkner's lesser works, or of his purpose in writing it, "Tomorrow" does capture that sense of a profound, complex, and intense existence of southern life identified with the best of Faulkner's fiction. Jackson Fentry, the "little, worn, dried-out hill man," surely qualifies for being the kind of heroic man found in Faulkner's works, as defined by critic-author-teacher Lionel Trilling: "A salient characteristic of William Faulkner's imagination is its preoccupation with conduct that is in the highest degree principled and magnanimous. Faulkner seems to take a special pleasure in representing men incapable of acting merely for their own advantage. . . . They appear again and again in Faulkner's novels and stories as representatives of the ideal of personal honor."[3] Fentry is a man of pride, humility, and uncomplaining endurance, traits Faulkner admires because, as he once said, they make "human life worthwhile, give it dignity."[4] If, indeed, Faulkner wrote "Tomorrow" as a potboiler, he nevertheless produced a moving story of love. He could not withhold his enormous talent.

Although the story stands on its own as an effective work of short fiction, it gains more significance as a part of American literature because it is an early entry into Faulkner's fictional world of Yoknapatawpha County. It introduces Gavin Stevens, twenty-eight-year-old Uncle Gavin in the story, who later appears in Faulkner's Yoknapatawpha stories where, according to one critic, he often serves as the author's "more or less proprietory wise man and choric overvoice."[5]

"Tomorrow" is described by Faulkner's biographer, Joseph Blotner, as a "detective story of character and fate, rather than fact." Faulkner elevates the story from the usual standards of the genre by establishing the integrity of his detective. The narrator mentions that Uncle Gavin was educated at Harvard and Heidelberg, signifying that he is a man of letters and intellectual depth. Later, when he recalls his uncle's visit with the Pruitts and what they told him, he says, "It was as if people looked at his face and knew that what he asked was not just for his own curiosity or his own selfish using." Through Faulkner's Uncle Gavin, as with the ancient Greek storytellers before him, the "spirit of inquiry meets the spirit of poetry and tragedy is born."[6] The title itself is of course an echo from one of Shakespeare's great tragedies.

"Tomorrow" is a tale told in the oral tradition ("Tell me," "Tell it," "Tell," Uncle Gavin urges those he seeks out to tell him about Fentry.) The story is pieced together on front porches, storefronts, and from hearsay and eavesdropping. Chick, Uncle Gavin's nephew, now an adult, tells what he remembers as a boy of twelve and intersperses his telling with the recollections of three of Fentry's neighbors. At least one critic has noted Faulkner's complex narrative style has no "cinematic equivalent." One of the fascinating aspects of our comparative inquiry was discovering how the creators of the motion-picture version of "Tomorrow" overcame this seemingly unsolvable problem of multiple narrators.

Although Faulkner does not set down the events in chronological order, readers have no trouble keeping clear the time and sequence of the bits and pieces of the plot—the causal relationships of the characters and events. Reading a story is usually a voluntary, solitary experience that gives readers control of time, place, and surroundings. They can pick up the magazine or book and read it whenever or wherever they like, staying with it at their own pace, starting and stopping at will, rereading or skipping any part they wish to. In film and live television (before the advent of home video recorders) the story continues uninterrupted, except for TV commercials. Reading, therefore, allows time for on-the-spot, unhurried contemplation and reflection and personal association—when the boy is taken away, readers can pause and relate Fentry's response to their own involvement with loss. The act of reading is a tactile, hands-on experience; readers can actually hold, clutch, clip, tear, or throw away the medium and the content. Print is a past-tense medium. The story we read has already taken place. As we shall see, live television and film are, with a slight difference between them, present-tense forms. Readers are both more isolated and more insulated than are viewers of the other two media. At the same time, however, readers have considerable freedom for imagination and personal participation. In print the words create the images. And because inner-eye visions are unlimited and permit readers unrestricted creative leeway, they are, in "Tomorrow," for instance, not locked into Faulkner's representation of Fentry as one of those men "who seem to become old men at fifty and then become invincible to time." Many readers, regardless of region, create a picture of their own invincible Fentry. But TV and film audiences are forced to accept the casting choices as the media's "poetic license."

Faulkner's use of the nephew Chick as the prime narrator, telling the tale in retrospect and further filtering the telling through the other tellers, sifts out sentimentality, purifies the deepest feelings, and gives the story a sense of freshness: what we are reading for the first time is being told for the first time. Chick, after twenty years, is telling it now because he can at last put it all together. He now understands, as his Uncle Gavin did within twenty-four hours, the why of it. "Of course he [Fentry] wasn't going to vote Book-wright free," Uncle Gavin said. The mature man, Chick, can relate to what his uncle meant on the drive back from Frenchman's Bend, when Gavin so forcefully insisted: "And you wouldn't have freed him either. Don't ever forget that. Never."

"Tomorrow" is more profoundly appreciated if we think of it as a mythic tale. It goes beyond facts and the mere recitation of exposition and incidents to support a preconceived effect. As a mythic tale, it takes on the Faulknerian pursuit of wisdom and truth: it seeks to understand the "human heart in conflict with itself." In spite of the hardships and human loss that Jackson Fentry suffers, he, like Faulkner's other plain people (or "tall men," as he calls them) still dreams, still holds on to the promise of tomorrow.

We never meet Fentry directly in the story, though he is the protagonist. He is a silent man with hidden passions, and it may be that we could not learn anything from him anyway. We do, through the narrators, get an outsider's introspection of Fentry's behaviour and learn how he set the events of the story in motion and eventually why. In this way we see Fentry as a symbol of the little man acting heroically. In his defiance he emerges as a man who will remain invincible even in the anguish and travail of frustration.

Jackson Fentry is a complex character. When we first come upon him he seems a taciturn man with simple tastes, simple emotions, and rigid principles. He is a plain man of the soil, farming on a plot of hill land that is too poor and too small. "His pa and his grandpa worked it," his neighbor Pruitt relates, "made a living for themselves and raised families and paid their taxes and owed no man. I don't know how they done it, but they did." Pruitt further explains that Jackson Fentry lost his mother early, just as Fentry's father had lost his. Both women had been killed by "that place" before they were forty. We are told that Fentry never thought of marrying. "How can a man afford to marry," Pruitt asks, "when him and his pa have just one pair of shoes between them?"

But as the tale unfolds we discover Fentry's capacity for love and his pride of heritage, and he becomes a man of large proportions capable of compassion and sacrifice. When the boy is taken away from him by his dead wife's brothers, he accepts the loss, determined to live with it by seemingly putting the boy out of his mind. Some years later, Pruitt asks him what happened to the boy, whether he had died, and Fentry answers, "What boy?" Yet, years after that, when he hears that the boy is grown, is now named Buck Thorpe, and has become a drunk and a brawling bully, he gets on his mule and rides thirty miles to see him. He finds him drinking and fighting. After watching silently from a distance, we are told, "he turned the mule and rid back up the road toward them hills he hadn't ought to never have left. Except maybe it's like the fellow says, and there ain't nowhere you can hide from either lightning or love." We know then that Fentry did not, could not, forget the boy who once was his son. The male child, in the southern tradition, means continuity of land and family. The boy and tomorrow and hope, which are inseparably linked, constitute the mythic structure of the story.

In "Tomorrow" as in almost all of his fiction, Faulkner cannot escape the memory of "the tragic fable of Southern history."[7] Fentry names the boy Jackson and Longstreet for the two generals of the lost war because he tells Pruitt, "Pa fit under both of them." It is not an act of defiance but an affirmation—a commemoration of what the Faulkner scholar M. E. Bradford describes as "the fierce and often barefoot 'cavalry' brigades who stood firm in the face of the grapeshot at Manassas and made endless forced marches under the command of the original Stonewall—the slaveless men to whom 'the war' had been an invasion."[8] In this churchless baptizing, Fentry is expressing the hope that the boy will grow up in the spirit and tradition of those illustrious Confederate commanders.

Faulkner fills the tale with the tone and atmosphere of the rural South. The boy, like the Fentry men before him, is chopping cotton as soon as he can walk. "But you couldn't see the boy at all; you could just see the cotton shaking where he was." Captain Stevens, Gavin's father, takes his nap every afternoon after dinner; Mrs. Pruitt, wearing " a clean gingham sunbonnet," sits on the gallery shelling field peas into a wooden bowl"; and Isham Quick is seated on the gallery "while the cicadas shrilled and rattled in the trees . . . talking in a lazy sardonic voice, like he had all night to tell it in." Vivid imagery is one of Fualkner's hallmarks as a short-story writer.

The class distinctions of the Deep South are spelled out early in the story when Chick explains that Uncle Gavin could talk to a jury "so that all the people in our country—the Negroes, the hill people, the rich flatland plantation owners—understood what he said." And conventional bigotry of the time and place is expressed in the voice of the narrators without condescension or explanation: when Fentry worked at the Quick sawmill, Isham Quick explains, he was "doing the same work and drawing the same pay as the niggers."

Fentry's capacity for love in this version of "Tomorrow" is made explicit only in his feelings about the boy. Faulkner only implies Fentry's feelings toward the boy's mother, "his wife," the "black-complected" woman with "pretty durn ruthless blood pride." Horton Foote, as he tells us, was fascinated by this nameless woman and she became a major character in his dramatic versions.

Faulkner does not give too much attention to women in his stories of the plain people. But from *Light in August* the experience of Lena Grove, also pregnant when she falls into the hands of Byron Bunch, we can assume a parallel possibility. Like Byron, perhaps Fentry did fall in love with the woman he identified as his wife. Because of her condition, a man with Fentry's strong sense of honor and responsibility would take care of her because she would be dependent upon him. In any case, whatever love he felt for her was channeled into his love for the boy.

Although it is Fentry's great capacity to love that is the dominant theme in "Tomorrow," Professor James Newcomb has pointed to an attendant theme: "Man's relationship to the law, and the limits of that law." This thematic development, Newcomb explained, "begins in the first sentence of the story and goes on where Gavin Stevens, attempting to sway the jury to a position all but one of them held before the trial started, tells them that the law can only go so far. Although Stevens's summation is not the cause of Fentry's oak-strong determination, the speech validates his refusal to be drawn into the will of the jury. The defendant's own attorney has told them a man must do what he has to do, pointing out that Bookwright solved his problem 'to the best of his ability and beliefs, asking help of no one, and then abode by his decision and his act.'"

Uncle Gavin's father, Captain Stevens, alerts the reader that law and Fentry's attitude about it are relevant in solving the mystery of why one man of twelve voted against acquittal. "Well, Gavin," he says with undisguised irony, "at least you stopped talking in time to hang just your jury and not your client." What Fentry, like Captain Stevens, hears in Gavin's summation is that a man sometimes has to rise above the law in order to obtain justice.

This is not to suggest that Faulkner is advocating anarchy or encouraging civil disobedience. Buck Thorpe, who flaunts the law for nefarious reasons, is killed. Bookwright, who kills him, turns himself in—willing to accept the law's judgment. Gavin Stevens, as a lawyer, is an officer of the court. And apparently Fentry has always acceded to the law. ("The only time Jackson and that boy was separated as much as one full breath," Pruitt explains, "was once a year when Jackson would ride in to Jefferson to pay their taxes.") But so strong within him were his deeply felt human passions and beliefs that Fentry's choice was inevitable. "I can't help it," he tells the other jurors who are trying to persuade him, "I ain't going to vote Mr. Bookwright free."

Only when Chick, the Pruitts, and Isham Quick finish telling the reader about Fentry and the "wife" who died and the boy he took as his son is it clear that the intensity of his love dominates all of his actions, including his adherence to the letter of the law.

We see, ultimately, that "Tomorrow" is a worthy representation of William Faulkner's talents and deserves consideration as part of his epic Yoknapatawpha cycle. It fits into the Faulkner pattern, what M. E. Bradford calls his "hard-won and hard-headed optimism about the human future." This faith in the human spirit was, according to Bradford, "based upon his discovery of the Jackson Fentrys among the lowly of the earth."

In "Tomorrow" we also see the skill of Faulkner as a writer of the short story, a form which this author who called himself a "failed poet" rated above the novel in his hierarchy of literary values. This mythic tale, composed in the genre of escapism, has unity of theme, tone, and mood, all bound together by a strong, articulate style. Faulkner's technique and his control of the material are masterful, all the more so because they are seemingly effortless.

A short story's communication with the reader is completed when the true nature of the hero is revealed. This revelation, or "epiphany" as James Joyce termed it, takes place for the readers of "Tomorrow" when they solve the mystery of Jackson Fentry's capacity for undeviating love and his determination to "endure and endure and then endure, tomorrow and tomorrow and tomorrow."

THE LIVE TELEVISION DRAMA

The first and most startling change to be noted in tracing the transformation of a literary work from the printed page to the screen, whether television or movie, is the shift in the number of creative people involved in the process. That number can change from one, the author, to literally hundreds as the various artistic talents and technological skills required by the new medium become part of the creative effort. In the case of "Tomorrow"'s transition to television, the idea began with a producer, Herbert Brodkin, who suggested to an actor-turned-playwright, Horton Foote, that Faulkner's story might be the basis for a drama to be performed live on Playhouse 90. This highly regarded series had, for five years, been presenting the popular live teledramas that uniquely characterized the legendary (but then waning) Golden Age of Television. And "Tomorrow," destined to become one of Playhouse 90's final offerings, would also become a fine example of the live drama form at its best.

How does a writer begin an adaptation? Horton Foote, recalling his work on "Tomorrow," offered some insights in our interviews with him. Initially he was reluctant to take on the adaptation. "Old Man," another Faulkner story which he had previously dramatized for Playhouse 90, had made quite an impact and Foote felt that producers were merely following the Hollywood syndrome: Lightning struck once, let's try it again. Moreover, as a playwright in his own right, Foote understandably has a preference for his own work. The writer of an original work, he says, can draw on unconscious material. Adaptation requires a more conscious effort to seek out and develop a dramatic structure for narrative elements which may be quite complex in prose form.

It was his fascination with that shadowy figure the "black-complected" woman in Faulkner's story that finally led Foote to his adaptation of "Tomorrow." While pondering the woman's fate, he found that the unconscious chemistry that occurs in preparing an original work had taken hold of him. He then had to mold this inspiration to fit a very peculiar and still developing medium: live television. Whether or not he was conscious of it, Foote's efforts, and later those of his collaborators, as we shall see, would be shaped by the fact that no storytelling form ever devised can offer such a massive heterogeneous, yet paradoxically intimate audience as that provided by television.

From its inception, television had been regarded as a sort of electronic fireplace, a place for person-to-person communication, including the telling of stories. And it soon became apparent that the stories this new, instantly transmitted medium tells best are those that are intimate, intense, aimed at the emotions. For television immediately exhibited some still familiar characteristics, both imposed and inherent. Its programs are organized in boxed-in time slots of thirty, sixty, ninety, or more minutes. They are beamed through prescribed channels to individual viewers who are alone or in a small group, sitting or reclining, close to the small screen, usually in familiar, comfortable, and small-scale surroundings. The television viewer is not part of the crowd, but *the* crowd. And each one at no cost has the best seat in the house.

No wonder, then, that the live television drama, which by necessity compresses and consolidates plot, people, and place into a tight frame, turned out to be the ideal fit for the snug home-screen viewing environment. And Faulkner's tale of a simple Mississippi man of the earth gave Foote all the right ingredients for an effective live teledrama. The televised adaptation of "Tomorrow" fittingly begins on a front porch and then moves into Jackson Fentry's sparse boiler-room living quarters. In this indoor, confined, and implosive ambience he and the woman (now named Sarah) meet, eat, sleep, keep warm, talk, and reach *in* to each other. On the day after the first showing of the live TV "Tomorrow," various TV critics in their mostly favorable reviews noted how effectively the adaptation demonstrated the tenderness, compassion, and patience of Fentry, especially in the scenes where this man of lifelong solitude acts out "flashes of sweetness" and "noblest instincts" toward Sarah and the boy who is the child of another man. We understand how the at-home viewer, observing in close-up, is stirred by the intensity of this "untutored, uncomplicated" cotton farmer with his patched shirt and meager belongings, whose inner resources enable him to sustain even after Sarah's death the hope that love brings to him. And we can assume, almost on the strength of the critical comments alone, that this "Tomorrow," in its new form, has remained true to the original in its essence.

Although the live television play is the youngest of the story-telling genres, and still not bound by tradition, it clearly has several of the same essential characteristics as does the short story: one main theme, an uncomplicated plot, few characters, undeviating narrative drive, and consistency in mood, tone, and language. At the same time, live television telling is a different distinctive medium, and its audience participates in a new and unique viewing experience.

Live television drama is truest to its form and potential when its forceful immediacy captures people "live," illuminates character—when it shows us faces: Sarah's contentment as she huddles close to the warming wood-burning stove; the monosyllabic, un-blinking Fentry's look of humility when he blurts out, "Marry me, Sarah"; Papa Fentry's immediate, contained, but unquestioning show of compassion in welcoming home Fentry and the motherless baby boy. Live television's finest moments are when its technology speaks simply and its close-up lens explores human emotions. In "Tomorrow," for instance, Sarah tells Fentry why she won't ever go back home to her papa who ordered her out of his house because she married Eubanks. "My Papa has his pride; and I've got mine," she says, and the accompanying close-up shot gives us a significant slice of her emotional biography. The camera x-rays feelings dramatically at the end of the play when Pruitt asks Fentry what happened to the boy who has been gone for some years and Fentry stoically answers, "What boy?" In print this scene of deep emotion withheld touches the reader. In the sight and sound medium it packs a wallop.

Television has been defined as compact communication, "a microscope not a telescope." The television telling of "Tomorrow" hits home hard because the microscope reveals motivation. The smaller-than-life people who are pinpointed for us are convincing and lifelike when we electronically peer into their faces and discover their inner reasons for doing what they do. Film, of course, also focuses within. But, here again, live television and big-screen film have a different territorial imperative. The film screen which Herbert Zettl, a theorist in TV aesthetics, tells us we look *at*, offers a vista for action; the television screen which Zettl says we look *into*, gives us a mirror for reaction. On this point, an early leading TV dramatist, Rod Serling, wrote, "The facial study on a small screen carried with it a meaning and power far beyond its usage in the motion pictures."[9]

Aided by what Henry James calls "the pressure of the spoken word," which was not available to the reader of Faulkner's story, the visual Playhouse 90 version of "Tomorrow" chronicles Fentry's welling love for Sarah: he gives her his coat against the "raw and cold" winter wind soon after he discovers her; to bring her hard candy for Christmas, he walks miles to the store while she sleeps in his bed; he shares with her his dream of a house of his own. The hovering, scanning camera, in exacting the long-nesting inner drives of this solitary man and in making his actions and silences visually articulate, validates and enhances the mood, tone, and theme of Faulkner's prose. We know why this gentle, considerate, independent, resolute man will take care of Sarah's baby, "like he was my own." We believe what we see in print because it first impresses us logically. It stimulates the mind. We believe what we see and hear in the graphic media because it first reaches us emotionally. It pumps the heart.

In order fully to understand the unique characteristics of the live television drama genre when compared with either print or film, we need to acknowledge that American commercial television is first, foremost, and fundamentally an advertising medium. This fact of electronic life which most of us have learned to live with, however begrudgingly, is important because it affects how the plays are put together and how we view them. Faulkner followers who wanted to read "Tomorrow" in 1940 needed only to buy the 23 November issue of the *Saturday Evening Post* for five cents. Faulkner-Foote-film buffs who wanted to see the film version in 1972 needed only to buy a ticket at the box office for around $2.00. (Alas, not many did.) Television viewers in 1960 (and again in 1961) who wanted to tune in to "Tomorrow," starring Richard Boone and

Kim Stanley, did not have to pay anything. This live play, which cost $113,000 to make, was on the air because its sponsors (who paid an additional sum of around $113,000) hoped to persuade the millions of viewers to buy Camel cigarettes and All-State insurance, and to patronize "Your Gas Company" and assorted local establishments, including, in the Los Angeles area, the Santa Anita race track.

In other ways, too, television viewing differs from any other communication experience. The nonpaying home viewer, unlike the ticket-buying, congregated seat-holder for film, theater, and other public arts, has the authority to turn off the performance at any time. He also has unrestricted mobility in his "auditorium," as does the reader. But the TV viewer, especially of a once-only, continuously performed live drama, unlike the prose reader, cannot stop or start, re-view or peek ahead. (Home video is, of course, changing this, transforming both film and video into a more "literary" medium, one in which viewers can check out titles, collect a personal library, savor again and again their favorite moments in any order they choose.)

Although readers, like the viewers of live TV, are isolated and unattended and their attentions are unpredictable, these unhampering conditions are more critical in the TV viewing environment. Is the set on? Is anybody watching it? If so, how attentively? While "Tomorrow" was being shown, various viewers were no doubt reading, paying bills, knitting, writing letters, eating, dozing off; or the phone may have rung, nature called, the baby awakened. Frequently, television audiences received a startling "tease" at the beginning of a live drama. This was a sometimes outrageous, even desperate attempt to keep viewers sitting still. Upon first reading the script for "Tomorrow," the television director requested "more theatrical excitement" in the opening scenes. This remark suggests the director's concern for matching Foote's quiet drama with the medium's fragile hold over the viewer.

For the creators of live network drama, the overall most imposing demand, the biggest bugaboo is TIME. The commitment of, to, and for time is television's holiest of holies. No other medium is as scrupulous in its obedience to the clock's precise second as is television (and, of course, its progenitor and model, radio). And the rule of time, in its several manifestations, affects the live drama genre more profoundly than its visual cousins, film and tape.

The writer in live television constructs the play with the tick of the clock as collaborating guide and master. The script must tell the story within the irrevocable time limit allowed—for the ninety-minute Playhouse 90, seventy-two minutes. And most important—

and to novices, most challenging—the script is fashioned so that approximately every fifteen minutes the story reaches a cliff-hanger, making way for the commercial breaks, which generally run anywhere from thirty seconds to two minutes, after which the script has to rekindle the mood and tone and restore the narrative drive.

This and other conventional strictures of time are illustrated by Horton Foote's experience in adapting "Tomorrow" for the small screen, beginning with the urgency of producer Herbert Brodkin's request that he agree to undertake the dramatization. "I hadn't remembered reading it, although I had read most of Faulkner's stories," Foote explains. "I found myself interested yet hesitant because the story seemed a little gimmicky to me, like a kind of detective story. But as is the way with television, they were most anxious to have a quick decision from me. I knew Brodkin and liked the work he did, so I went for a long walk along the Hudson River, near my home in Upper Nyack, to see if I could find a way to tackle the dramatization.

"As I walked along the river, the character of the woman became alive to me, even though Faulkner gives only a few paragraphs to her. He told me enough about her so that my imagination just began to work, and she became somebody I knew. I began somehow in the most obsessive, vivid kind of way to want to discover for myself, as a writer, what went on between Jackson Fentry and this 'black-complected' woman. It's interesting to note that both actresses who played her—Kim Stanley in television and Olga Bellin in film—are blonde. But they both understood the fierce pride of the woman, 'black-complected blood pride' Faulkner calls it. I was very intrigued by the character of Fentry—mainly because of the humanity of the man—but I got into the story because I became fascinated by who the woman was who was in the cabin with him, and what her story was. Why was she in the cabin? Why did she marry Fentry? What was her past?

"And so that night I sat down and I began to dramatize what I felt was the story of Jackson Fentry and this woman Faulkner never names. I called her Sarah and had her married to a man named Eubanks. I worked on that element of the story that night and finished it the next morning. And from that day until this, I have never changed it."[10]

Five days later Foote finished his adaptation and six weeks after that, 7 March 1960, it went on the air. "Tomorrow" got the highest ratings Playhouse 90 had achieved in two years, claiming in its three successive half-hour periods an Arbitron share-of-audience (percentage of viewers with sets on) ranging from 32.5 to 39.2.

One particular time problem for Horton Foote was that Faulkner's story is not told in sequence and covers a period of more than twenty years. "I decided," Foote explains, "that what I had to address myself to was dramatizing, as best I could, the story Faulkner had given me and let the director and the producer take care of solving the time-change problems in their casting of my play."[11] To make the somewhat diffused chronology of the story clearer for the once-only viewer, Foote began his play with the search of the lawyer, Gavin Stevens, now Thornton Douglas. (His name and those of others in the story had to be changed in both the TV and film versions, since a movie company owned the rights to the names.) In this way, Horton Foote kept the story's original spine, the pursuit of the same mystery: why Jackson Fentry can't vote Bookwright free.

Also, instead of three of the characters telling their stories to Douglas and his nephew (now Charles) narrating them together with his own recollections, Foote confined his narration to the Pruitts. "It was apparent," he says, "that given the character of Fentry, Stevens would never go directly to him, and I felt that my structure—the relationship between Fentry and Sarah—would be best served by one point of view, one narrator, if you will." So these choices—the choice of where to begin the story, the choice of dramatizing very fully the relationship of Sarah Eubanks and Jackson Fentry, the choice of the Pruitts as narrators, the choice of trying to accommodate in some way Faulkner's time structure—all dictated the form that evolved as the first dramatized version of "Tomorrow."

Foote remembers that director Robert Mulligan, who in 1954 had directed two Faulkner adaptations, "Smoke" and "Barn Burning," on the thirty-minute live Suspense series, asked him to try a rewrite, starting with the trial and building the story from there. "He liked what I had done but he felt that the beginning lacked theatrical excitement—a term I've heard often in my television life. I had earlier thought of starting with the trial but, given the seventy-two minutes actually allotted for playing time, it had seemed to me uneconomical use of the time. I tried. However, after a few days, which was all the time we had to work on changes, we agreed it was no improvement over my beginning and we returned to what I had already written. But I did start the film version with the trial."

Another unalterable time factor in live television is that action, as in theater but not in film and print, takes place in real time. This is of most concern to the director. Robert Mulligan, in staging the live "Tomorrow," could not "cheat" Fentry across the room to go out and get firewood in less time than it takes Richard Boone as Fentry to make the move. In film the director has the option of having Fentry crossing the room in a few seconds or less—the actor steps towards the door and a cut shows him at the woodpile or even reentering with the wood in his arms. Or, if desired for pace, suspense, or plot development, the move to the woodpile or wherever can take many minutes or longer by intercutting or flashback. Live television's real-time rigidity often arbitrarily arranges for the author the sequence of scenes as well as determining which characters appear on camera and when. If an actor requires any difficult change in dress or in appearance (in age or physical look), or cannot readily get from the ending of one scene to the opening of the next, the script or the director must devise some stage business to cover the interim. (The commercial break does sometime come to the rescue.)

In the opening daytime scene of "Tomorrow" the Pruitts, mother and son, are sitting on their porch talking about Fentry to Uncle Thornton and Charles. At the end of the scene, and as Pruitt starts his on-camera flashback narration, a dissolve takes us to Fentry and his father twenty years before, silently eating together in their cabin. (Richard Boone does not look like a twenty-year-old, but as Faulkner wrote, at that age Fentry was "already looking forty.") Then, as Pruitt continues his voice-over narration, "One night . . . in the summer of nineteen-two . . ." the camera pans slowly back to the Pruitt porch, which has by now been lit for night. The pan gives Fentry real time to go from his cabin outside to the porch, where he now has a scene with Mrs. Pruitt. He tells her, "I got me a job over at the sawmill at Frenchman's Bend." In Faulkner's story Fentry gives this information to the son. But the son cannot appear in the scene; he has to continue with his narration and so is off-camera. Director Mulligan handled the twenty-year switchback in age for Mrs. Pruitt by shooting her mostly in a wide two-shot and keeping her in the background of the darkened-for-night scene. This composition makes dramatic sense, too, because our attention here should be and is on Fentry, who is in the foreground of the two-shot as well as in full front view in single shots.

Another constriction is the matter of preparation time—a thorny period for actors, designers, costumers, and others, but most prickly for the director of the live television play. The director is the Big Daddy of the production, responsible for everything that goes on the air. As Paddy Chayefsky, one of the most successful of the live drama writers for television, testified, the director "has a complex and frightening job."[12] Yet, he is given short shrift in the time allotted to plan and prepare the play. This is in sharp contrast to today's practices. Most present-day film directors, usually see the script well before the shooting begins, sometimes spending many months working closely with producers, writers, designers, actors, and others, planning, revising, polishing and developing a director's plot covering staging and interpretation. George Roy Hill, who was a sought-after TV drama director before going to Hollywood, said after directing the film *Butch Cassidy and the Sundance Kid* that seeing a film from conception to distribution takes from two to five years out of a director's life.

For the live TV director the preproduction time is always scarce, always harried, and sometimes nonexistent. The TV director seldom reads the finished script until at most a few weeks, sometimes not until a few days or even hours, before it goes into rehearsal. It was not uncommon, especially in the Golden Age of live drama, the early 1950s, for a sought-after director such as Robert Mulligan—now also a prominent film director—to end a show one night, start on the next show the following morning, spend a day or two on casting, and then begin rehearsals.

The director's job can be divided into two principal concerns, both related to time. First, to regulate traffic, making sure that the lights, cameras, microphones, music, sound effects, sets, and actors are all where they're supposed to be at the exact same time. Second, to be absolutely certain that the presentation begins and ends on the precise second, so that the eighteen minutes of commercials and promotion spots and station breaks will be given their full time priority. The director always knows—and if he doesn't, the producer or the network representative, and most assuredly the sponsor's agency executive will make sure he knows—that if the play takes too much time, the script is to be cut, never the commercials.

"Tomorrow" was aired live except for taped inserts of the leading players at the opening and the shots of the baby. During rehearsals three scenes were cut in order to pare the show down to its allotted time: Fentry at the store buying the hard candy, Sarah's burial, and Fentry milking the goat. All three scenes were put back in the film version.

More than directors in any other storytelling form, live TV directors have to come equipped with a built-in sense of time and an ability to adapt to it. During an on-the-air performance the director in the control room, situated with assistants and technical crew above and away from the studio floor, has to be a quick-on-the-draw, one-shot artist, always ready and able to improvise in case of errors of either commission or omission from any or all involved. Dramatist Rod Serling once defined, with appreciation, the director's lot during air time. "At that point where the legitimate play director quietly steals off into the darkness in the rear of the theater to entrust his work to the opening night cast—this is when the television director works the hardest in the most trying, frenetic, inhuman tension imaginable. He's an obstetrician assisting at a birth, but he's also nurse, anesthetist, and general manager of the hospital."[13]

In addition, directors of live television drama, more so than film directors, have to be speed-reading visualists, able to have 20/ 20 foresight, to envision in their mind's eye how the scene will show up on the small screen. They must be adept at instant, impromptu assembling. Directors of live drama edit the play in the camera. And they have very little time, especially as compared with film directors, to rehearse with cameras—in the case of "Tomorrow," only for the last three of the sixteen rehearsal days. Thus, Robert Mulligan could not indulge himself with spending too much time in the seven-hour rehearsal day working with actors on interpretation or experimenting with various camera angles. Yet he had to be finely tuned to the rhythms and styles of the actors and camera persons in order to set the staging and call his shots at air time.

For the makers, as it is for the viewers, live television is a "now only" medium, a "no chance again" phenomenon. No chance to look at the dailies, as in film, or to revise in the editing room. No chance, as in theater, to see how it plays under the lights in New Haven. No chance, as in publishing, to correct the galleys before publication.

For viewers, too, live drama was and remains mostly a once-only opportunity. The live TV version of "Tomorrow," like the vast majority of the over 5,000 such live presentations, is presently not available for any kind of showing, and probably will never be. A film copy of the Playhouse 90 production is in the CBS vaults, but complicated permission rights make its release just about impossible.

The unalterable present-tense pressures of the live genre conspired to make it the most critically collaborative medium of all: a simultaneous synthesis. Each person involved in putting the play on the air—from the seen actors to all the unseen specialists in the studio and control room and other cubicles, including the solitary engineer at the transmitter who dispatches the picture the audiences will view—has to be in tune with the spirit and on cue with the letter of the script. At the same time.

The tyranny of time is probably felt most severely and personally by the actor, who is the most exposed member of the ensemble. Actors seldom get the script until a few days before rehearsals (when they are cast), and often not until rehearsals begin. They have to learn their lines and stage business and get into their characters and interpretations with very little help from the director or anyone else. For the actor especially, speed is the method in this electronic madness. Yet this extra edge of pressure is what probably gives live TV drama its single most important and distinguishing virtue—its remarkable sense of immediacy. For the good actors the tension of time in getting the show ready for air more often than not brought out performances that were more intense, more of a piece.

The two leads in the television adaptation of "Tomorrow," Kim Stanley as Sarah and Richard Boone as Fentry, gave matching affecting performances even though they apply their craft in different ways. Kim Stanley is a "method" actress who works on an analytical level, calling on her life experience to bring to the surface her actions. She augments her dialogue with small details—gestures, expressions, eye movement, and much touching of furniture, clothing, and her body—to reveal to the audience that she is thinking and feeling. Richard Boone, who had to overcome his rugged western image as the hired gun Paladin in the successful television series *Have Gun Will Travel,* is more a result actor. He played Fentry with sincerity, stressing the man's humility and making him sympathetic without seeming to engage in psychoanalysis. They both succeeded, however, in welding their highly individual styles to the needs of the drama and gave performances that the *New York Times* called "warm, genuine and poignant."

To those who took part in the excitement of the transitory live television drama—now, because of tape and film, a rare TV happening—the fact that so many teleplays were done as well as they were, under the restrictions of time and in the medium's particular atmosphere of terror and tension, is miraculous. Gore Vidal, in making this point, does so as a writer, but what he says connects to all the collaborators: "I discovered that although the restrictions imposed by a popular medium are not always agreeable, they do at least make creative demands upon one's talents and, more often than not, the tension between what one is not allowed to say and what one *must* say creates ingenious effects which, given total freedom, might never have been forced from the imagination."[14]

Horton Foote agrees and, recalling his experience in adapting "Tomorrow," adds: "For me, drama in its best sense is a form of concentration. I have found that sometimes limitations are a great asset. One of the great hindrances is an overindulgence, having too much to choose from, too much to work with. Sometimes when you are forced to be economical, especially in the setting, and through compressing your material, the characters, and the plot, you can clarify and intensify the drama.

"I wouldn't have known how to do 'Tomorrow' except the way that I did it, and although I'm not close in form, I feel I'm close in essence to Faulkner's story. I think there has to come a point in adaptations where another chemistry has to come in. I don't really think you serve the original by being too literal or by trying to withhold your own chemistry. What Faulkner has given us in his 'Tomorrow' is a mythic story and like all myths you can retell it and redo it in many different ways and still retain the original power and universality of the myth."[15]

THE FILM

When producers Gilbert Pearlman and Paul Roebling, who had been mainly involved in New York theater, decided to film "Tomorrow," they wanted to make "the most stunningly beautiful movie of a Faulkner work that's ever been done."[16] Previously, Faulkner novels had turned into screen failures. *The Sound and the Fury, The Story of Temple Drake, Sanctuary,* and *The Long Hot Summer* were largely dismissed by critics as too heavily melodramatic, while *The Reivers* was called "pleasant but insubstantial." The best of the lot was *Intruder in the Dust,* admirably produced and directed by Clarence Brown and filmed on location in and near Oxford, Mississippi, in 1949. Faulkner's own time in the Holywood sun as a screenwriter had only a few bright moments.

The two producers were originally inspired to make "Tomorrow" into a film by an experimental stage production in 1968 of Horton Foote's live television adaptation, imaginatively directed by Herbert Berghof in his New York City theater school studio. In particular, they wanted film repeats of performances by Olga Bellin (Roebling's wife) as Sarah Eubanks, and Robert Duvall as Jackson Fentry, which were centerpieces of the stage version. When *Tomorrow* was released in 1972, there was a positive critical and audience response to the interpretation of these two roles, typified by one critic's hailing of Robert Duvall's "flawless re-creation of Faulkner," aided, another critic said, by "the superlative quality of Olga Bellin's performance." The actor himself to this day considers Jackson Fentry to be one of his finest roles. Both Duvall and Bellin attribute the development of their performances in the film to their earlier participation on the stage of the Berghof studio. However, according to the actress, shooting the film on location aided considerably in enhancing the sense of reality and gave her an opportunity to improve the "southernness" of her speech.

But *Tomorrow* was a total flop at the box office. A serious blow came quickly when Vincent Canby of the *New York Times*, a vitally influential film critic, especially for any off-the-beaten-track film, gave it a negative review. He criticized it, among other reasons, because the filmmakers had supplied no "cinematic equivalent" to the distancing device provided by Faulkner via the multiple narrators of the story. Joseph Anthony, the film's director, disputed this in his comments to us, suggesting at least one equivalent: the choice of black and white instead of color. The film's gray tones serve as a filter for emotions that rich, unnaturally vivid film color would have sentimentalized. A second filter was the restrained and uncomplicated direction by Anthony, his concentration on the performances—an approach reverently captured on camera by Alan Green, director of photography. The intensity and believability of a performance can, as it does in *Tomorrow*, affect the emotional impact on an audience in a most profound way. As Reva Schlesinger, the film's editor, told us, "No scriptwriter could predict what Bob Duvall can do with a scene."[17] She particularly mentions Duvall's skill in conveying "emotional violence," recognizing this actor's ability to make inner feelings visible in a profound way—the ability that prompted one critic a few years later to call him "the American Olivier."

Duvall's portrayal and the inspired performances of the other professionals in the cast, together with Joseph Anthony's uncluttered, sensitive direction and the decision of the producers to film on location, casting local residents in character roles, brings an immediate and compelling authenticity to the film adaptation. These are some reasons why, when *Tomorrow* was first released, it was called, in contradiction to Canby's dissenting view, "one of the best independent productions in the recent history of American narrative film."[18]

Nevertheless, *Tomorrow* faded away from the general public's view soon after its initial spotty theatrical release in 1972. The film, however, did not stay completely out of sight or mind. Indeed, it became a born-again cinema event when some eleven years later it was re-released in theaters and the once box-office flop turned a financial flip. This independently produced film, made with fidelity and devotion by its collaborators, had been kept alive through the years because of enthusiastically-received showings at film festivals, college classrooms, and Faulkner symposiums, and it was inspired to renewed life because of the emergence of a Robert Duvall "cult." Critics and media interviewers would usually refer to *Tomorrow* when commenting on Duvall's growing stature as an actor, always identifying his Jackson Fentry portrayal, as the actor himself would, as his best screen work of all of his thirty roles. Specifically, in early 1983, when Sheila Benson, film critic for the *Los Angeles Times,* reviewed *Tender Mercies,* the fourth of Duvall's film vehicles written by Horton Foote, a film for which each won Academy Awards, she understandably recalled the earlier Foote-Duvall *Tomorrow* collaboration. Assessing Duvall's Fentry role, she wrote, "Never has a performance been so fiercely championed and so little seen by the moviegoing public." Benson went on to compare Duvall's newest role of Mac Sledge, an ex-country songwriter, to his earlier performance of the Mississippi dirt farmer, calling his portrayal of Sledge "the other half of a bracket in the proud career of Robert Duvall . . . His Mac Sledge is fit to stand with Jackson Fentry as a work of great simplicity, dignity, and insight."[19] The Benson review with its generous references to the rounded excellence of *Tomorrow,* stirred a revival of the film around the country. It was released in the fall in theaters in Beverly Hills, San Francisco, New York, and other cities, getting rave reviews once more, making a good run wherever it played, and bringing a delayed but substantial return to its faith-keeping producers. It has since been shown on cable television, the PBS network, and is available for home cassette sale and rental. This film, like other classic works in the medium and like Faulkner's own written creations, has its own rendezvous with perpetuity.

Producing a narrative on film, as on live TV, is a collaborative process, almost always fixed and unchangeable. The writer's script and the performer's interpretations are ultimately shaped and locked in for all time in the final cut made by the editor, usually under the supervision of the director and/or producer. In *Tomorrow,* coproducer Roebling was involved in every phase of the production, from gathering props, sets, and money straight through to editing of the final scene. Roebling's determination throughout not to compromise on aesthetic principles resulted in a "No deal" for any kind of Hollywood financing and distribution. Had he not come up with over $600,000 from personal assets, the adaptation process for *Tomorrow* would have most likely come to a halt at the Berghof studio.

This kind of commitment and willingness to treat tragic themes is more usually identified with the European film tradition. *Tomorrow,* which one critic called the closest thing to Greek tragedy that has been done on film, is an addition to that small number of serious American films of quality which include *Citizen Kane, The Informer, Grapes of Wrath,* and *A Streetcar Named Desire.* It is a film which, because its makers had the wit and courage not to ignore Faulkner but to tap into his literary power, in the words of another reviewer, "stands majestically among the best American art films."[20]

Wherefore an art film? From its very beginning in this country, the business of film was not art but business. And the men who made it a prosperous business, in the best American tradition of profit and private enterprise, were immigrants.

In the early years of this century, eastern Europeans such as Adolph Zukor, Samuel Goldwyn, Carl Laemmle, and William Fox, came to this country and eventually made their way to California to pursue the American dream. Making and selling motion pictures, creating a totally new American industry that collectively became known as Hollywood, gave them the chance to realize their visions of gold and glory and glamour for themselves. These pioneering operators of the penny arcades and nickelodeons soon founded, built, and controlled Hollywood production studios, nationwide film exchanges, and movie palaces, and made and distributed films the public liked. They themselves were the public. They instinctively understood the fantasy world of motion pictures and they erected rococco theaters to accommodate their make-believe products. And because these men loved the business of making films, and wanted to insinuate into their stories American visions and values, they occasionally permitted—sometimes even encouraged—filmmakers such as Frank Capra, John Ford, and Howard Hawks to turn out quality films, especially when these films could also become good box-office films. For the most part, however, the movie moguls made films that made money and also brought them social and even political power and prestige.

For almost forty years Hollywood dominated the film industry—90 percent of all American movies were made there—and these adventuresome mythmakers from Germany, Hungary, Poland, and Russia dominated Hollywood. They became the American Film Establishment.

But in the late 1940s and early 1950s a series of severe quakes shook the Hollywood industry, subsequently dislodging the tycoons and dismantling their dynasties. A government antitrust order forced a separation of studio ownership from ownership of theaters. The once-bountiful foreign market for Hollywood films fell off. And most devastating of all was "that damn little box" in the living room. The American habit of going to the movies—some 90 million moviegoers a week in 1946—gave way to staying at home to watch Milton Berle and "I Love Lucy" and the live TV dramas on Kraft Television Theatre, Philco-Goodyear Television Playhouse, Studio One, and Playhouse 90.

At the beginning of the 1970s, as we come to the era of the film *Tomorrow,* the name of the game was the same but Hollywood was a different ball park. New landlords were in charge. Instead of the zealous visionaries with "show biz" in their blood—the Founding Immigrants—the new managers of the Big Studios were the icy-veined ministers of the Big Conglomerates. It was, as it is today even more so, the time of The Deal. And mostly The Big Deal. And to this day The Deal is considered Hollywood's highest art form.

It was in this new climate that producers Pearlman and Roebling set out to make their movie. They soon learned that if they wanted to film their Faulkner-Foote story the way they had in mind—in black and white, with no box-office names, a downbeat tale of a poor Mississippi cotton farmer, and with no redeeming sex or violence—no studio in Hollywood would make a deal. Nevertheless, they went ahead. With faith and fidelity, and on a shoe-string (Roebling's), they determined they would make the most stunningly beautiful movie of a Faulkner work that had ever been made. And, fortunately, the transition from stage to film was made easier because Horton Foote was not only available but anxious to do the screen adaptation.

"A film has its own rhythm, its own life," Foote tells us.[21] In transposing "Tomorrow" into film, he had, as he says, "a concept about a beginning, a middle and end for it that was aesthetically pleasing and dramatically sound."[22] To keep his narrative drive clear and in sequence, he made Uncle Gavin, now lawyer Thornton Douglas, the story's sole narrator, a choice that echoed Faulkner's later concept. As we have mentioned, in Faulkner's Yoknapatawpha stories this Harvard- and Heidelberg-trained lawyer often becomes the proprietory wise man and choric overvoice.

Foote also knew that in shaping his live TV story for film he could take advantage of film's incredible fluidity. The film camera is an omniscient author. It can record any action wherever and however the director directs. It can tell the story as narrator from an objective point of view or subjectively represent the point of view of any one character or several characters; it can record stream of consciousness; it can itself become a character in the story; and it can take any one or any combination of these points of view in the same film. Film allows for flashbacks, parallel action, and visualizing the future, but essentially what we see happening on the screen seems to be happening now. Yet film is not as immediate, as truly present-tense, as broadcasting. The present tense of film falls, as Gilbert Seldes stated, "somewhere between the past of fiction and the immediate present of broadcasting." The basic unit in film is the shot, the length of time the camera continues taking the picture. Through optical effects created in the laboratory, film has a variety of transition devices. The most basic ones include the cut (an immediate change from one shot to another), fade-out (the shot gradually disappears into blackness), fade-in (the shot gradually appears out of darkness), and dissolve (the second shot gradually appears as the first shot gradually disappears). Film is a series of still pictures projected usually at twenty-four frames per second to give the illusion of motion—motion pictures.

In the opening few minutes of *Tomorrow,* as the printed credits are intermittently superimposed over the action on the screen, the director keeps his camera in almost constant motion as he gives us necessary plot exposition and introduces us to the setting and to Fentry, the story's protagonist. We can observe in the beginning scenes many of the innate characteristics and techniques of the motion picture form and at the same time perceive where it differs from print and from live television.

We first see Fentry in the rear row of the jury box and he appears as Faulkner describes him, "frail and work-worn." We next see him in the jury room. He is in a corner by himself and the exasperated jury foreman pleads with him to go along with the other eleven members of the jury and vote Bookwright free. The camera next cuts to Fentry in a close-up, and Fentry says, "I can't help it. I ain't going to vote Bookwright free." Lawyer Douglas begins his narration, but the camera holds on the grim, unmoving, unshaven Fentry. The lawyer's first words tell us what the story is going to be about. "And so, Jackson Fentry, cotton farmer, hung my jury. Who was he?" The close-up dissolves into a close-up of Fentry twenty years before, clean-shaven and vigorous looking. Then the camera follows Fentry walking down a country road, passing a house or two and a country store with some people sitting out in front. Music of the rural South comes in, a hymn which starts low in moderate tempo but picks up in volume and tempo as Fentry strides to his job at the sawmill. After Isham leads him to his boiler-room living space, a montage (a series of overlapping shots) shows Fentry's daily routine as he settles in at the sawmill—shaving, washing clothes, whittling, sleeping. We see that he has brought a certain order to the squalor of his existence. The credits are completed. It is now the day before Christmas and the mystery-drama of why Fentry can't vote Bookwright free is about to unfold.

During those first minutes—which in film belong to the director—we see how, unlike live television which is locked into real time and space, the motion picture creates its own time and space; how it can break the action into many parts, holding each for as long as it needs to, and at various angles and distances within the frame;

how film makes simultaneous use of picture, speech, motion, sound, music, place, silence, and light and dark. We also see how film, like live television, controls the attention of the spectator by showing as much (Fentry and the other jurors) or as little (Fentry alone) as is necessary and by the selection of shots indicating who is experiencing what at any given moment. Mike Nichols, a highly successful director in stage and film, has explained the difference between the two media: "In a movie the camera has to *choose one person.* That's one of the crucial differences."[23]

Both live television and film make crucial choices for the viewer. But the live teledrama can only put on its viewer's small screen what any one of its two, three, and sometimes four cameras are able to capture as an action happens. Film, usually using only one camera, is an *ex post facto* medium. What its camera sees can be edited. Sergei M. Eisenstein, the great Russian director and film theorist, succinctly described what film editing is: Show a girl with a look of horror and if the next shot is a lion we understand her fear. But show a mouse and we laugh. Because of editing, the filmmaker can manipulate the content, arrange the order, restructure the story line, insert special effects and key lighting, add music and sound, and, as many actors know, leave scenes on the cutting-room floor. Editing makes film, as a medium, closer to print than to live television. The filmmaker, under the best of circumstances, is like the writer who can rewrite and rewrite and rewrite.

Both film and live TV, the senior and junior members of the visual media, have their roots of content and method not just in literature but also in the other older arts of drama, dance, painting, sculpture, architecture, and music. The borrowed elements of picture composition, continuity of story line, rhythm, tone, and language have enabled film technology to develop its own technique and do more than make still pictures create an illusion of motion. As in *Tomorrow*, a film can capture the internal and external life of people; it can fill its frames with actions, intentions, feelings, dreams, fears and hopes of its moving images. It can tell a story *and* make a statement about the human condition.

When Sarah wakes up the first morning in Fentry's cabin, we hear the sound of wood being chopped outside. She is in pain, but she struggles to get out of bed. She goes to the mirror. We know she is not the kind of woman who is used to checking her appearance. As she primps her hair, the camera cuts to Fentry outside chopping wood. This arrangement of shots tells us much about their relationship after only twenty-four hours together. We see them reassuming their long unused roles of female and male. To help us realize that feminine-masculine vibes are stirring in the chilly Mississippi air, instrumental music starts up and Sarah holds her hand up to the window where the sunlight is streaming in. She takes off her blouse and washes her upper body, above the slip she is wearing, another indication of her wish, her need to feel like a woman, to feel clean. Fentry comes in carrying the wood for the stove. The music fades out. Quickly, but with no alarm or embarrassment, she turns her back to him and puts her blouse back on.

This scene is crucial, not only to the plot line—will she stay or go?—but in telling us how the film will treat their relationship. Their love will not manifest itself in any demonstrative physical contact.

In real life we seldom see a scene the way a film camera shows it to us. A high angle shot or an extreme close-up, for example. Or an over-the-shoulder and into-the-face view. Film creates its own reality. We accept the film experience because we accept film as a metaphor. Its symbols create its language. The film lens pinpoints the specific to extend the message. Sarah's smile as she sits in front of the warming fire tells us she will stay. Fentry chopping the wood and tending the fire tells us he will take care of her.

When people started telling stories, not too much attention was given to details of setting; the stories were mostly about human beings and animals and the gods. When the written tradition took on storytelling, more attention was paid to details and to symbols. But film, as critic Stanley Kauffmann wrote, strips from fiction "the primary function of creating material reality. The film has not only taken over this function but exalted it: it manages to make poetry out of doorknobs, breakfasts, furniture. Trivial details, of which everyone's universe is made, can once again be transmuted into metaphor, contributing to imaginative art."[24]

In *Tomorrow*, a safety pin contributes to one of the most poignant scenes in the film. Fentry and Sarah are sitting in the warm sun on the grass in the clearing in the woods talking about a house that Fentry hopes to build there. She reminisces about a "fine house" she once wanted to live in and tells him that her father's house had no trees or grass, "there was nothing." Then she laughs and lies down on the grass and exclaims, "I love grass and flowers and trees." We see her, for the first and only time, joyful. She then sits up, unfastens a safety pin on Fentry's shirt and repins it to cover a larger tear. And she gently touches his shoulder. This is the strongest and most explicit love scene in the film. It is followed immediately by the sun going behind a cloud "casting a shadow over the earth."

Sarah pulls her shawl around her; it is her shroud. We know their love is doomed.

While film and live TV are both fastidious *internalizers* capable of extracting and transmitting the emotional, film is better able to pursue revelation in yet another dimension. Film is the best of all the storytelling media in *externalizing* inner tensions, hopes and doubts, expectations and confusions. It can deal with a physical environment in ways that live TV, theater, and even print and oral storytelling cannot. Because it can open up the action, create a vista, go in and out of Fentry's cabin at will, for instance, it increases its vocabulary. It commands more symbols and more metaphors, most of which are universal. Film's visual language, with the help of dubbing and subtitles, can be understood by almost all of the world's peoples, in a world where the number of spoken and written languages totals more than four thousand.

A scene in *Tomorrow* illustrates the universality of film's in-and-out mobility, which enables spectators, no matter what their native language, to perceive more than meets the eye. Sarah and Fentry, after they have been together for about a month, are sitting in the cabin at night and it is raining outside. The talk between them is gloomy. She goes on about floods, Jesus walking on water, and concludes, "They say God is gonna destroy the world next time by fire." Then she goes to the window, looks out, and a dissolve shows daytime, spring flowers, and Sarah seated in a chair outside the cabin watching Fentry as he boils clothes in a large iron pot. She is in good spirits. "It's much warmer today," she says. "It'll be spring before you know it." And she wonders about her baby, "if it's going to be a boy or girl."

These two connecting sequences tell us a great deal about what has happened to their relationship in the month they have been together. It is now intimate and easy; they trust each other. However, we sense a foreboding in Sarah she cannot shake, no matter how warming the sun or how comforting Fentry's attentions. And because the film has shown us Fentry's life, in its physical and emotional settings, we empathize with his need and desire to make their relationship permanent. We root for him when in the outdoor scene, as he continues to stir the clothes in the pot, he proposes for the first time.

In whatever form stories take, the events are closest to the truth when they come out of what the teller knows. But when reaching for art, the teller must disclose more than facts. William Faulkner did that in his "Tomorrow." Horton Foote did that in both of his adaptations of the mythic tale. Foote, in his versions, took over a set of facts: Sarah is carrying a baby, and though Fentry is not the father, he promises her he will take care of the boy, "like he was my own." But that is not the full reality of the situation, that is not the stuff of a mythic tale. These facts alone do not expose the universal center of their experience—the passion, yearning, loneliness, dignity, pride, and love that Sarah and Fentry discover and support in each other in their time together. Nor do facts alone reveal the "inexhaustible voice" within this man of silence who, because he has a soul, is awakened by his love for Sarah and the boy. What else is demanded, and what Faulkner, Foote, et al. supplied, is insight and instinct, that mysterious but dynamic duo that stirs memory and stimulates imagination. "I trust instinct absolutely, though it is blind and dumb," the philosopher Bertrand Russell once said.[25] And he later observed that when Albert Einstein discovered relativity, he began with a kind of "mystical or poetical insight into truth."[26]

Most creative people cannot and do not try to explain the chemistry of individual or ensemble creativity. Also inexplicable is the way to go about finding the absolutely right mix of content and form for a work when it is transformed into another medium. It is easier to discover what does not work than it is to discern what will.

However, when we explore comparative media, we find that certain characteristics, techniques, and technologies are exclusive to each storytelling medium, even as some are common to all and are interchangeable. And when a story such as "Tomorrow" is told in three different forms we observe how the individualized components of each medium will impinge mightily upon the nature and shape of the story's content. But, in the end, we are most struck not by the several differences of the three media but by their astonishing potential, their common imperative. For the three "Tomorrow"'s convince us that each medium, in its own fashion, can evoke universal truths about the human condition and in so doing bring beauty, harmony, meaning, and hope even to the lowly and invincible of the earth.

"The poet's voice," William Faulkner said in ending his Nobel Prize acceptance speech, "need not merely be the record of man, it can be one of the props, the pillars to help him endure and prevail."

We believe that the poet's voice speaks to that end in "Tomorrow" and "Tomorrow" and *Tomorrow*.

David G. Yellin
Marie Connors

1. Faulkner to Bennett Cerf, July 24, 1940, in *Selected Letters of William Faulkner,* ed. Joseph Blotner (New York: Random House, 1977), p. 134.

2. Faulkner to Robert K. Haas, April 28, 1940, in *Selected Letters,* p. 121.

3. Lionel Trilling, *The Experience of Literature* (Garden City: Doubleday & Company, p. 745.

4. M. E. Bradford, "Faulkner's 'Tomorrow' and the Plain People," *Studies in Short Fiction,* 2 (1965): 236.

5. Bradford, p. 239.

6. Edith Hamilton, *The Greek Way* (New York: W. W. Norton & Company, 1942), p. 228, quoting W. Macneile, *Tragedy,* p. 51.

7. James Newcomb, lecture, Memphis State University, Memphis, Tenn., 5 October 1978.

8. Bradford, p. 237.

9. Rod Serling, *Patterns* (New York: Simon & Schuster, 1955), p. 10.

10. Horton Foote, interview with authors, New York, N.Y., 19 October 1978.

11. Horton Foote, "*Tomorrow:* The Genesis of a Screenplay," *Faulkner, Modernism and Film,* Faulkner and Yoknapatawpha, *1978,* eds. Evans Harrington and Ann J. Abadie (Jackson: University Press of Mississippi, 1978), p. 157.

12. Paddy Chayefsky, *Television Plays* (New York: Simon & Schuster, 1955), p. 259.

13. Serling, p. 40.

14. Gore Vidal, *Visit to a Small Planet* (Boston: Little, Brown & Co., 1956), p. xiv–xv.

15. Foote interview.

16. Paul Roebling, interview with authors, New York, N.Y., 25 May 1979.

17. Reva Schlesinger, interview with authors, 6 May 1979.

18. Bruce F. Kawin, *Faulkner and Film* (New York: Ungar, 1977), p. 65.

19. Sheila Benson, "Robert Duvall's Vein of Troubled Loneliness," *Los Angeles Times,* 6 March 1983, p. 21.

20. Rex Reed, "Forget the Awards but Don't Miss Tomorrow," *New York Daily News,* 14 April 1972, p. 62.

21. Foote, p. 161.

22. Foote interview.

23. Mike Nichols, quoted in Barbara Gelb, "Mike Nichols: the Special Risks and Rewards of the Director's Art," *New York Times Magazine,* 27 may 1984, p. 38.

24. Stanley Kauffmann, "The Film Generation," *The Emergence of Film Art,* ed. Lewis Jacobs (New York: Hopkinson and Blake, 1969), p. 425.

25. Bertrand Russell, quoted in Robert Alden, "Advertising: A Form or a Delicate Art?" *New York Times,* 7 May 1961, sec. 3, p. 14.

26. Ibid.

I
THE SHORT STORY

TOMORROW
William Faulkner

This illustration by Floyd Davis accompanied Faulkner's story when it was originally published in The Saturday Evening Post *on 23 November 1940.*

UNCLE GAVIN had not always been county attorney. But the time when he had not been was more than twenty years ago and it had lasted for such a short period that only the old men remembered it, and even some of them did not. Because in that time he had had but one case.

He was a young man then, twenty-eight, only a year out of the state-university law school where, at grandfather's instigation, he had gone after his return from Harvard and Heidelberg; and he had taken the case voluntarily, persuaded grandfather to let him handle it alone, which grandfather did, because everyone believed the trial would be a mere formality.

So he tried the case. Years afterward he still said it was the only case, either as a private defender or a public prosecutor, in which he was convinced that right and justice were on his side, that he ever lost. Actually he did not lose it—a mistrial in the fall court term, an acquittal in the following spring term—the defendant a solid, well-to-do farmer, husband and father, too, named Bookwright, from a section called Frenchman's Bend in the remote southeastern corner of the county; the victim a swaggering bravo calling himself Buck Thorpe and called Bucksnort by the other young men whom he had subjugated with his fists during the three years he had been in Frenchman's Bend; kinless, who had appeared overnight from nowhere, a brawler, a gambler, known to be a distiller of illicit whiskey and caught once on the road to Memphis with a small drove of stolen cattle, which the owner promptly identified. He had a bill of sale for them, but none in the country knew the name signed to it.

And the story itself was old and unoriginal enough: The country girl of seventeen, her imagination fired by the swagger and the prowess and the daring and the glib tongue; the father who tried to reason with her and got exactly as far as parents usually do in such cases; then the interdiction, the forbidden door, the inevitable elopement at midnight; and at four o'clock the next morning Bookwright waked Will Varner, the justice of the peace and the chief officer of the district, and handed Varner his pistol and said, 'I have come to surrender. I killed Thorpe two hours ago.' And a neighbor named Quick, who was first on the scene, found the half-drawn pistol in Thorpe's hand; and a week after the brief account was printed in the Memphis papers, a woman appeared in Frenchman's Bend who claimed to be Thorpe's wife, and with a wedding license to prove it, trying to claim what money or property he might have left.

I can remember the surprise that the grand jury even found a true bill; when the clerk read the indictment, the betting was twenty to one that the jury would not be out ten minutes. The district attorney even conducted the case through an assistant, and it did not take an hour to submit all the evidence. Then Uncle Gavin rose, and I remember how he looked at the jury—the eleven farmers and storekeepers and the twelfth man, who was to ruin his case—a farmer, too, a thin man, small, with thin gray hair and that appearance of hill farmers—at once frail and work-worn, yet curiously im-perishable—who seem to become old men at fifty and then become invincible to time. Uncle Gavin's voice was quiet, almost monotonous, not ranting as criminal-court trials had taught us to expect; only the words were a little different from the ones he would use in later years. But even then, although he had been talking to them for only a year, he could already talk so that all the people in our country—the Negroes, the hill people, the rich flatland plantation owners—understood what he said.

'All of us in this country, the South, have been taught from birth a few things which we hold to above all else. One of the first of these—not the best; just one of the first—is that only a life can pay for the life it takes; that the one death is only half complete. If that is so, then we could have saved both these lives by stopping this defendant before he left his house that night; we could have saved at least one of them, even if we had had to take this defendant's life from him in order to stop him. Only we didn't know in time. And that's what I am talking about—not about the dead man and his character and the morality of the act he was engaged in; not about self-defense, whether or not this defendant was justified in forcing the issue to the point of taking life, but about us who are not dead and what we don't know—about all of us, human beings who at bottom want to do right, want not to harm others; human beings with all the complexity of human passions and feelings and beliefs, in the accepting or rejecting of which we had no choice, trying to do the best we can with them or despite them—this defendant, another human being with that same complexity of passions and instincts and beliefs, faced by a problem—the inevitable misery of his child who, with the headstrong folly of youth—again that same old complexity which she, too, did not ask to inherit—was incapable of her own preservation—and solved that problem to the best of his ability and beliefs, asking help of no one, and then abode by his decision and his act.'

He sat down. The district attorney's assistant merely rose and bowed to the court and sat down again. The jury went out and we didn't even leave the room. Even the judge didn't retire. And I remember the long breath, something, which went through the room when the clock hand above the bench passed the ten-minute mark and then passed the half-hour mark, and the judge beckoned a bailiff and whispered to him, and the bailiff went out and returned and whispered to the judge, and the judge rose and banged his gavel and recessed the court.

I hurried home and ate my dinner and hurried back to town. The office was empty. Even grandfather, who took his nap after dinner, regardless of who hung and who didn't, returned first; after three o'clock then, and the whole town knew now that Uncle Gavin's jury was hung by one man, eleven to one for acquittal; then Uncle Gavin came in fast, and grandfather said, 'Well, Gavin, at least you stopped talking in time to hang just your jury and not your client.'

'That's right, sir,' Uncle Gavin said. Because he was looking at me with his bright eyes, his thin, quick face, his wild hair already beginning to turn white. 'Come here, Chick,' he said. 'I need you for a minute.'

'Ask Judge Frazier to allow you to retract your oration, then let Charley sum up for you,' grandfather said. But we were outside then, on the stairs, Uncle Gavin stopping half-way down, so that we stood exactly halfway from anywhere, his hand on my shoulder, his eyes brighter and intenter than ever.

'This is not cricket,' he said. 'But justice is accomplished lots of times by methods that won't bear looking at. They have moved the jury to the back room in Mrs. Rouncewell's board-inghouse. The room right opposite that mulberry tree. If you could get into the back yard without anybody seeing you, and be careful when you climb the tree—'

Nobody saw me. But I could look through the windy mulberry leaves into the room, and see and hear, both—the nine angry and disgusted men sprawled in chairs at the far end of the room; Mr. Holland, the foreman, and another man standing in front of the chair in which the little, worn, dried-out hill man sat. His name was Fentry. I remembered all their names, because Uncle Gavin said that to be a successful lawyer and politician in our country you did not need a silver tongue nor even an intelligence; you needed only an infallible memory for names. But I would have remembered his name anyway, because it was Stonewall Jackson—Stonewall Jackson Fentry.

'Don't you admit that he was running off with Book-wright's seventeen-year-old daughter?' Mr. Holland said. 'Don't you admit that he had a pistol in his hand when they found him? Don't you admit that he wasn't hardly buried before that woman turned up and proved she was already his wife? Don't you admit that he was not only no-good but dangerous, and that if it hadn't been Bookwright, sooner or later somebody else would have had to, and that Bookwright was just unlucky?'

'Yes,' Fentry said.

'Then what do you want?' Mr. Holland said. 'What do you want?'

'I can't help it,' Fentry said. 'I ain't going to vote Mr. Bookwright free.'

And he didn't. And that afternoon Judge Frazier dis-charged the jury and set the case for retrial in the next term of court; and the next morning Uncle Gavin came for me before I had finished breakfast.

'Tell your mother we might be gone overnight,' he said. 'Tell her I promise not to let you get either shot, snake-bit or surfeited with soda pop. . . . Because I've got to know,' he said. We were driving fast now, out the northeast road, and his eyes were bright, not baffled, just intent and eager. 'He was born and raised and lived all his life out here at the very other end of the country, thirty miles from Frenchman's Bend. He said under oath that he had never even seen Bookwright before, and you can look at him and see that he never had enough time off from hard work to learn how to lie in. I doubt if he ever even heard Bookwright's name before.'

We drove until almost noon. We were in the hills now, out of the rich flat land, among the pine and bracken, the poor soil, the little tilted and barren patches of gaunt corn and cotton which somehow endured, as the people they clothed and fed somehow endured; the roads we followed less than lanes, winding and narrow, rutted and dust choked, the car in second gear half the time. Then we saw the mailbox, the crude lettering: G. A. FENTRY; beyond it, the two-room log house with an open hall, and even I, a boy of twelve, could see that no woman's hand had touched it in a lot of years. We entered the gate.

Then a voice said, 'Stop! Stop where you are!' And we hadn't even seen him—an old man, barefoot, with a fierce white bristle of mustache, in patched denim faded almost to the color of skim milk, smaller, thinner even than the son, standing at the edge of the worn gallery, holding a shotgun across his middle and shaking with fury or perhaps with the palsy of age.

'Mr Fentry—' Uncle Gavin said.

'You've badgered and harried him enough!' the old man said. It was fury; the voice seemed to rise suddenly with a fiercer, an uncontrollable blaze of it: 'Get out of here! Get off my land! Go!'

'Come,' Uncle Gavin said quietly. And still his eyes were only bright, eager, intent and grave. We did not drive fast now. The next mailbox was within the mile, and this time the house was even painted, with beds of petunias beside the

steps, and the land about it was better, and this time the man
rose from the gallery and came down to the gate.

'Howdy, Mr. Stevens,' he said. 'So Jackson Fentry hung
your jury for you.'

'Howdy, Mr. Pruitt,' Uncle Gavin said. 'It looks like he
did. Tell me.'

And Pruitt told him, even though at that time Uncle
Gavin would forget now and then and his language would slip
back to Harvard and even to Heidelberg. It was as if people
looked at his face and knew that what he asked was not just for
his own curiosity or his own selfish using.

'Only ma knows more about it than I do,' Pruitt said.
'Come up to the gallery.'

We followed him to the gallery, where a plump,
whitehaired old lady in a clean gingham sunbonnet and dress
and a clean white apron sat in a low rocking chair, shelling
field peas into a wooden bowl. 'This is Lawyer Stevens,' Pruitt
said. 'Captain Stevens' son, from town. He wants to know
about Jackson Fentry.'

So we sat, too, while they told it, the son and the mother
talking in rotation.

'That place of theirs,' Pruitt said. 'You seen some of it
from the road. And what you didn't see don't look no better.
But his pa and his grandpa worked it, made a living for themselves and raised families and paid their taxes and owed no
man. I don't know how they done it, but they did. And Jackson was helping from the time he got big enough to reach up
to the plow handles. He never got much bigger than that
neither. None of them ever did. I reckon that was why. And
Jackson worked it, too, in his time, until he was about twenty-
five and already looking forty, asking no odds of nobody, not
married and not nothing, him and his pa living alone and
doing their own washing and cooking, because how can a man
afford to marry when him and his pa have just one pair of
shoes between them. If it had been worth while getting a wife
a tall, since that place had already killed his ma and his
grandma both before they were forty years old. Until one
night—'

'Nonsense,' Mrs. Pruitt said. 'When your pa and me married, we didn't even own a roof over our heads. We moved into a rented house, on rented land—'

'All right,' Pruitt said. 'Until one night he come to me and said how he had got him a sawmilling job down at Frenchman's Bend.'

'Frenchman's Bend?' Uncle Gavin said, and now his eyes were much brighter and quicker than just intent. 'Yes,' he said.

'A day-wage job,' Pruitt said. 'Not to get rich; just to earn a little extra money maybe, risking a year or two to earn a little extra money, against the life his grandpa led until he died between the plow handles one day, and that his pa would lead until he died in a corn furrow, and then it would be his turn, and not even no son to come and pick him up out of the dirt. And that he had traded with a nigger to help his pa work their place while he was gone, and would I kind of go up there now and then and see that his pa was all right.'

'Which you did,' Mrs. Pruitt said.

'I went close enough,' Pruitt said. 'I would get close enough to the field to hear him cussing at the nigger for not moving fast enough and to watch the nigger trying to keep up with him, and to think what a good thing it was Jackson hadn't got two niggers to work the place while he was gone, because if that old man—and he was close to sixty then—had had to spend one full day sitting in a chair in the shade with nothing in his hands to chop or hoe with, he would have died before sundown. So Jackson left. He walked. They didn't have but one mule. They ain't never had but one mule. But it ain't but about thirty miles. He was gone about two and a half years. Then one day—'

'He come home that first Christmas,' Mrs. Pruitt said.

'That's right,' Pruitt said. 'He walked them thirty miles home and spent Christmas Day, and walked them other thirty miles back to the sawmill.'

'Whose sawmill?' Uncle Gavin said.

'Quick's,' Pruitt said. 'Old Man Ben Quick's. It was the second Christmas he never come home. Then, about the beginning of March, about when the river bottom at Frenchman's Bend would be starting to dry out to where you could skid logs through it and you would have thought he would be settled down good to his third year of sawmilling, he come home to stay. He didn't walk this time. He come in a hired buggy. Because he had the goat and the baby.'

'Wait,' Uncle Gavin said.

'We never knew how he got home,' Mrs. Pruitt said. 'Because he had been home over a week before we even found out he had the baby.'

'Wait,' Uncle Gavin said.

They waited, looking at him, Pruitt sitting on the gallery railing and Mrs. Pruitt's fingers still shelling the peas out of the long brittle hulls, looking at Uncle Gavin. His eyes were not exultant now any more than they had been baffled or even very speculative before; they had just got brighter, as if whatever it was behind them had flared up, steady and fiercer, yet still quiet, as if it were going faster than the telling was going.

'Yes,' he said. 'Tell me.'

'And when I finally heard about it and went up there,' Mrs. Pruitt said, 'that baby wasn't two weeks old. And how he had kept it alive, and just on goat's milk—'

'I don't know if you know it,' Pruitt said. 'A goat ain't like a cow. You milk a goat every two hours or so. That means all night too.'

'Yes,' Mrs. Pruitt said. 'He didn't even have diaper cloths. He had some split floursacks the midwife had showed him how to put on. So I made some cloths and I would go up there; he had kept the nigger on to help his pa in the field and he was doing the cooking and washing and nursing that baby, milking the goat to feed it; and I would say, "Let me take it. At least until he can be weaned. You come stay at my house, too, if you want," and him just looking at me—little, thin, already wore-out something that never in his whole life had ever set down to a table and et all he could hold—saying, "I thank you, ma'am. I can make out."'

'Which was correct,' Pruitt said. 'I don't know how he was at sawmilling, and he never had no farm to find out what kind of a farmer he was. But he raised that boy.'

'Yes,' Mrs. Pruitt said. 'And I kept on after him: "We hadn't even heard you was married," I said. "Yessum," he said. "We was married last year. When the baby come, she died." "Who was she?" I said. "Was she a Frenchman Bend girl?" "No'm," he said. "She come from downstate." "What was her name?" I said. "Miss Smith," he said.'

'He hadn't even had enough time off from hard work to learn how to lie either,' Pruitt said. 'But he raised that boy. After their crops were in in the fall, he let the nigger go, and next spring him and the old man done the work like they use to. He had made a kind of satchel, like they say Indians does, to carry the boy in. I would go up there now and then while the ground was still cold and see Jackson and his pa plowing and chopping brush, and that satchel hanging on a fence post and that boy asleep bolt upright in it like it was a feather bed. He learned to walk that spring, and I would stand there at the fence and watch that durn little critter out there in the middle of the furrow, trying his best to keep up with Jackson, until Jackson would stop the plow at the turn row and go back and get him and set him straddle of his neck and take up the plow and go on. In the late summer he could walk pretty good. Jackson made him a little hoe out of a stick and a scrap of shingle, and you could see Jackson chopping in the middle-thigh cotton, but you couldn't see the boy at all; you could just see the cotton shaking where he was.'

'Jackson made his clothes,' Mrs. Pruitt said. 'Stitched them himself, by hand. I made a few garments and took them up there. I never done it but once though. He took them and he thanked me. But you could see it. It was like he even begrudged the earth itself for what the child had to eat to keep alive. And I tried to persuade Jackson to take him to church, have him baptized. "He's already named," he said. "His name is Jackson and Longstreet Fentry. Pa fit under both of them."'

'He never went nowhere,' Pruitt said. 'Because where you saw Jackson, you saw that boy. If he had had to steal that boy down there at Frenchman's Bend, he couldn't 'a' hid no closer. It was even the old man that would ride over to Haven Hill store to buy their supplies, and the only time Jackson and that boy was separated as much as one full breath was once a year when Jackson would ride in to Jefferson to pay their taxes, and when I first seen the boy I thought of a setter puppy, until one day I knowed Jackson had gone to pay their taxes and I went up there and the boy was under the bed, not making any fuss, just backed up into the corner, looking out at me. He didn't blink once. He was exactly like a fox or a wolf cub somebody had caught just last night.'

We watched him take from his pocket a tin of snuff and tilt a measure of it into the lid and then into his lower lip, tapping the final grain from the lid with delicate deliberation.

'All right,' Uncle Gavin said, 'Then what?'

'That's all,' Pruitt said. 'In the next summer him and the boy disappeared.'

'Disappeared?' Uncle Gavin said.

'That's right. They were just gone one morning. I didn't know when. And one day I couldn't stand it no longer, I went up there and the house was empty, and I went on to the field where the old man was plowing, and at first I thought the spreader between his plow handles had broke and he had tied a sapling across the handles, untile he seen me and snatched the sapling off, and it was that shotgun, and I reckon what he said to me was about what he said to you this morning when you stopped there. Next year he had the nigger helping him again. Then, about five years later, Jackson come back. I don't know when. He was just there one morning. And the nigger was gone again, and him and his pa worked the place like they use to. And one day I couldn't stand it no longer, I went up there and I stood at the fence where he was plowing, until after a while the land he was breaking brought him up to the fence, and still he hadn't never looked at me; he plowed right by me, not ten feet away, still without looking at me, and he turned and come back, and I said, "Did he die, Jackson?" and then he looked at me. "The boy," I said. And he said, "What boy?"'

They invited us to stay for dinner.

Uncle Gavin thanked them. 'We brought a snack with us,' he said. 'And it's thirty miles to Varner's store, and twenty-two from there to Jefferson. And our roads ain't quite used to automobiles yet.'

So it was just sundown when we drove up to Varner's store in Frenchman's Bend Village; again a man rose from the deserted gallery and came down the steps to the car.

It was Isham Quick, the witness who had first reached

Thorpe's body—a tall, gangling man in the middle forties, with a dreamy kind of face and near-sighted eyes, until you saw there was something shrewd behind them, even a little quizzical.

'I been waiting for you,' he said 'Looks like you made a water haul.' He blinked at Uncle Gavin. 'That Fentry.'

'Yes,' Uncle Gavin said. 'Why didn't you tell me?'

'I didn't recognize it myself,' Quick said. 'It wasn't until I heard your jury was hung, and by one man, that I associated them names.'

'Names?' Uncle Gavin said. 'What na—Never mind. Just tell it.'

So we sat on the gallery of the locked and deserted store while the cicadas shrilled and rattled in the trees and the lightning bugs blinked and drifted above the dusty road, and Quick told it, sprawled on the bench beyond Uncle Gavin, loose-jointed, like he would come all to pieces the first time he moved, talking in a lazy sardonic voice, like he had all night to tell it in and it would take all night to tell it. But it wasn't that long. It wasn't long enough for what was in it. But Uncle Gavin says it don't take many words to tell the sum of any human experience; that somebody has already done it in eight: He was born, he suffered and he died.

'It was pap that hired him. But when I found out where he had come from, I knowed he would work, because folks in that country hadn't never had time to learn nothing but hard work. And I knowed he would be honest for the same reason: that there wasn't nothing in his country a man could want bad enough to learn how to steal it. What I seem to have underestimated was his capacity for love. I reckon I figured that, coming from where he come from, he never had none a-tall, and for that same previous reason—that even the comprehension of love had done been lost out of him back down the generations where the first one of them had had to take his final choice between the pursuit of love and the pursuit of keeping on breathing.

'So he come to work, doing the same work and drawing the same pay as the niggers done. Until in the late fall, when the bottom got wet and we got ready to shut down for the winter, I found out he had made a trade with pap to stay on until spring as watchman and caretaker, with three days out to go home Christmas. And he did, and the next year when we started up, he had done learned so much about it and he stuck to it so, that by the middle of summer he was running the whole mill hisself, and by the end of summer pap never went out there no more a-tall and I just went when I felt like it, maybe once a week or so; and by fall pap was even talking about building him a shack to live in in place of that shuck mattress and a old broke-down cookstove in the boiler shed. And he stayed through that winter too. When he went home that Christmas we never even knowed it, when he went or when he come back, because even I hadn't been out there since fall.

'Then one afternoon in February—there had been a mild spell and I reckon I was restless—I rode out there. The first thing I seen was her, and it was the first time I had ever done that—a woman, young, and maybe when she was in her normal health she might have been pretty, too; I don't know. Because she wasn't just thin, she was gaunted. She was sick, more than just starved-looking, even if she was still on her feet, and it wasn't just because she was going to have that baby in a considerable less than another month. And I says, "Who is that?" and he looked at me and says, "That's my wife," and I says, "Since when? You never had no wife last fall. And that child ain't a month off." And he says, "Do you want us to leave?" and I says, "What do I want you to leave for?" I'm going to tell this from what I know now, what I found out after them two brothers showed up here three years later with their court paper, not from what he ever told me, because he never told nobody nothing.'

'All right,' Uncle Gavin said. 'Tell.'

'I don't know where he found her. I don't know if he found her somewhere, or if she just walked into the mill one day or one night and he looked up and seen her, and it was like the fellow says—nobody knows where or when love or lightning either is going to strike, except that it ain't going to strike there twice, because it don't have to. And I don't believe she was hunting for the husband that had deserted her— likely he cut and run soon as she told him about the baby— and I don't believe she was scared or ashamed to go back home just because her brothers and father had tried to keep her from marrying the husband, in the first place. I believe it was just some more of that same kind of black-complected and not extra-intelligent and pretty durn ruthless blood pride that them brothers themselves was waving around here for about a hour that day.

'Anyway, there she was, and I reckon she knowed her time was going to be short, and him saying to her, "Let's get married," and her saying, "I can't marry you. I've already got a husband." And her time come and she was down then, on that shuck mattress, and him feeding her with a spoon, likely, and I reckon she knowed she wouldn't get up from it, and he got the midwife, and the baby was born, and likely her and the midwife both knowed by then she would never get up from that mattress and maybe they even convinced him at last, or maybe she knowed it wouldn't make no difference nohow and said yes, and he taken the mule pap let him keep at the mill and rid seven miles to Preacher Whitfield's and brung Whitfield back about daylight, and Whitfield married them and she died, and him and Whitfield buried her. And that night he come to the house and told pap he was quitting, and left the mule, and I went out to the mill a few days later and he was gone—just the shuck mattress and the stove, and the dishes and skillet mammy let him have, all washed and clean and set on the shelf. And in the third summer from then, them two brothers, them Thorpes—'

'Thorpes,' Uncle Gavin said. It wasn't loud. It was getting dark fast now, as it does in our country, and I couldn't see his face at all any more. 'Tell,' he said.

'Black-complected like she was—the youngest one looked a heap like her—coming up in the surrey, with the deputy or bailiff or whatever he was, and the paper all wrote out and stamped and sealed all regular, and I says, "You can't do this. She come here of her own accord, sick and with nothing, and he taken her in and fed her and nursed her and got help to born that child and a preacher to bury her; they was even married before she died. The preacher and the midwife both will prove it." And the oldest brother says, "He couldn't marry her. She already had a husband. We done already attended to him." And I says, "All right. He taken that

boy when nobody come to claim him. He has raised that boy
and clothed and fed him for two years and better." And the
oldest one drawed a money purse half outen his pocket and let
it drop back again. "We aim to do right about that, too—when
we have seen the boy," he says. "He is our kin. We want him
and we aim to have him." And that wasn't the first time it ever
occurred to me that this world ain't run like it ought to be run
a heap of more times than what it is, and I says, "It's thirty
miles up there. I reckon you all will want to lay over here
tonight and rest your horses." And the oldest one looked at

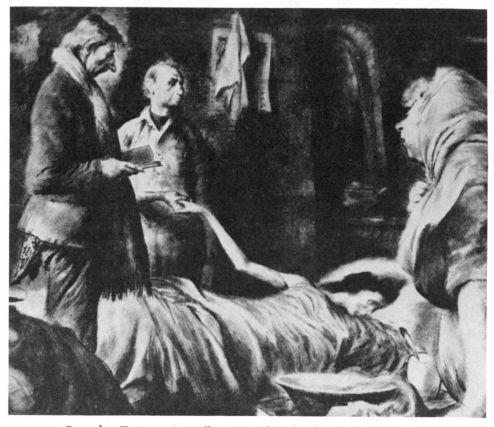

Saturday Evening Post *illustration by Floyd Davis depicts the mar-*
riage of Jackson Fentry and Sarah Eubanks.

me and says, "The team ain't tired. We won't stop." "Then I'm going with you," I says. "You are welcome to come," he says.

'We drove until midnight. So I thought I would have a chance then, even if I never had nothing to ride. But when we unhitched and laid down on the ground, the oldest brother never laid down. "I ain't sleepy," he says. "I'll set up a while." So it wasn't no use, and I went to sleep and then the sun was up and it was too late then, and about middle morning we come to that mailbox with the name on it you couldn't miss, and the empty house with nobody in sight or hearing neither, until we heard the ax and went around to the back, and he looked up from the woodpile and seen what I reckon he had been expecting to see every time the sun rose for going on three years now. Because he never even stopped. He said to the little boy, "Run. Run to the field to grandpap. Run," and come straight at the oldest brother with the ax already raised and the down-stroke already started, until I managed to catch it by the haft just as the oldest brother grabbed him and we lifted him clean off the ground, holding him, or trying to. "Stop it, Jackson!" I says. "Stop it! They got the law!"

'Then a puny something was kicking and clawing me about the legs; it was the little boy, not making a sound, just swarming around me and the brother both, hitting at us as high as he could reach with a piece of wood Fentry had been chopping. "Catch him and take him on to the surrey," the oldest one says. So the youngest one caught him; he was almost as hard to hold as Fentry, kicking and plunging even after the youngest one had picked him up, and still not making a sound, and Fentry jerking and lunging like two men until the youngest one and the boy was out of sight. Then he collapsed. It was like all his bones had turned to water, so that me and the oldest brother lowered him down to the chopping block like he never had no bones a-tall, laying back against the wood he had cut, panting, with a little froth of spit at each corner of his mouth. "It's the law, Jackson," I says. "Her husband is still alive."

'"I know it," he says. It wasn't much more than whispering. "I been expecting it. I reckon that's why it taken me so by surprise. I'm all right now."

' "I'm sorry for it," the brother says. "We never found out about none of it until last week. But he is our kin. We want him home. You done well by him. We thank you. His mother thanks you. Here," he says. He taken the money purse outen his pocket and puts it into Fentry's hand. Then he turned and went away. After a while I heard the carriage turn and go back down the hill. Then I couldn't hear it any more. I don't know whether Fentry ever heard it or not.

' "It's the law, Jackson," I says. "But there's two sides to the law. We'll go to town and talk to Captain Stevens. I'll go with you."

'Then he set up on the chopping block, setting up slow and stiff. He wasn't panting so hard now and he looked better now, except for his eyes, and they was mostly just dazed looking. Then he raised the hand that had the money purse in it and started to mop his face with the money purse, like it was a handkerchief; I don't believe he even knowed there was anything in his hand until then, because he taken his hand down and looked at the money purse for maybe five seconds, and then he tossed it—he didn't fling it; he just tossed it like you would a handful of dirt you had been examining to see what it would make—over behind the chopping block and got up and walked across the yard toward the woods, walking straight and not fast, and not looking much bigger than that little boy, and into the woods. "Jackson," I says. But he never looked back.

'And I stayed that night at Rufus Pruitt's and borrowed a mule from him; I said I was just looking around, because I didn't feel much like talking to nobody, and the next morning I hitched the mule at that gate and started up the path, and I didn't see old man Fentry on the gallery a-tall at first.

'When I did see him he was moving so fast I didn't even know what he had in his hands until it went "boom!" and I heard the shot rattling in the leaves overhead and Rufus Pruitt's mule trying his durn best either to break the hitch rein or hang hisself from the gatepost.

'And one day about six months after he had located here to do the balance of his drinking and fighting and sleight-of-hand with other folks' cattle, Bucksnort was on the gallery here, drunk still and running his mouth, and about a half dozen of the ones he had beat unconscious from time to time by foul means and even by fair on occasion, as such emergencies arose, laughing every time he stopped to draw a fresh breath. And I happened to look up, and Fentry was setting on his mule out there in the road.

'He was just setting there, with the dust of them thirty miles caking into the mule's sweat, looking at Thorpe. I don't know how long he had been there, not saying nothing, just setting there and looking at Thorpe; then he turned the mule and rid back up the road toward them hills he hadn't ought to never have left. Except maybe it's like the fellow says, and there ain't nowhere you can hide from either lightning or love. And I didn't know why then. I hadn't associated them names. I knowed that Thorpe was familiar to me, but that other business had been twenty years ago and I had forgotten it until I heard about that hung jury of yourn. Of course he wasn't going to vote Bookwright free. . . . It's dark. Let's go to supper.'

But it was only twenty-two miles to town now, and we were on the highway now, the gravel; we would be home in an hour and a half, because sometimes we could make thirty and thirty-five miles an hour, and Uncle Gavin said that someday all the main roads in Mississippi would be paved like the streets in Memphis and every family in America would own a car. We were going fast now.

'Of course he wasn't,' Uncle Gavin said. 'The lowly and invincible of the earth—to endure and endure and then endure, tomorrow and tomorrow and tomorrow. Of course he wasn't going to vote Bookwright free.'

'I would have,' I said. 'I would have freed him. Because Buck Thorpe was bad. He—'

'No, you wouldn't,' Uncle Gavin said. He gripped my knee with one hand even though we were going fast, the yellow light beam level on the yellow road, the bugs swirling down into the light beam and ballooning away. 'It wasn't Buck Thorpe, the adult, the man. He would have shot that man as quick as Bookwright did, if he had been in Bookwright's place. It was because somewhere in that debased and brutalized flesh which Bookwright slew there still remained, not the spirit maybe, but at least the memory, of that little boy, that Jackson and Longstreet Fentry, even though the man the boy had become didn't show it, and only Fentry did. And you wouldn't have freed him either. Don't ever forget that. Never.'

II
THE TELEVISION PLAY

TOMORROW
Horton Foote

*Kim Stanley and Richard Boone played the roles of Sarah Eubanks
and Jackson Fentry in the television play. (This photograph and
others in this section were made directly from the television screen.)*

FOLLOWING are cast and production credits for Playhouse 90's special production of William Faulkner's "Tomorrow," Monday, March 7, 1960, on the CBS Television Network:

ON AIR
9:30–11:00 PM, EST

ORIGINATION
Hollywood (live)

FORMAT
90-minute drama

STARS
Richard Boone, Kim Stanley, Chill Wills, Beulah Bondi, Elizabeth Patterson, and guest star Charles Bickford

CAST

Jackson Fentry	RICHARD BOONE
Sarah Eubanks	KIM STANLEY
Ed Pruitt	CHILL WILLS
Mrs. Hulie	BEULAH BONDI
Mrs. Pruitt	ELIZABETH PATTERSON
Pa Fentry	CHARLES BICKFORD
Les Thorpe	JAMES OLSON
Isham	ANDREW PRINE
Sheriff	WILLIAM CHALLEE
Charles Douglas	JIMMY BAIRD
Jackson and Longstreet	PETER OLIPHANT
Thornton Douglas	CHARLES AIDMAN
Bud Thorpe	ROBERT SORRELLS
The preacher	JOHN LORMER
Lee Masters	JOHN HAMBRICK
Buck Thorpe	RON NICHOLAS
Sam White	SAM EDWARDS
Pete	FRANK KILIMOND

PRODUCER
Herbert Brodkin

DIRECTOR
Robert Mulligan

WRITER
Adapted for Playhouse 90 by Horton Foote

ASSOC. PRODUCERS
Bob Markell and Russell Stonehamnm

ART DIRECTOR
Edgar Lansbury

MUSIC DIRECTOR
Jerry Goldsmith

ASSOCIATE DIRECTOR
Lennie Horn

LIGHTING DIRECTOR
Leard Davis

TECHNICAL DIRECTOR
Robert Stone

SPONSORS AND AGENCIES
American Gas Association, Lennen & Newell, Inc.; Allstate Insurance Co., Leo Burnett Co., Inc.; Camel Cigarettes, William Esty Co., Inc.

NETWORK PRESS REPRESENTATIVES
Archie Teague (Hollywood)
Jim Sirmans (New York)

ANNOUNCER
Dick Joy

THE SCRIPT for the television play "Tomorrow" printed here is a scene-by-scene transcription of the play as presented live on CBS Playhouse 90, March 7, 1960.

> *The voice of an off-camera announcer is heard over black screen.*

ANNOUNCER (VO)   March 7, 1960. Live. From Television City in Hollywood.

> *Playhouse 90 theme music begins with drum roll, and three revolving stars appear on black screen.*

ANNOUNCER (VO)   A special presentation on Playhouse 90.

> *The words "Playhouse 90" appear on screen. As the announcer introduces the cast brief individual shots of the six starring actors appear in a triangle over the program series logo. All are medium close-up shots.*

ANNOUNCER (VO)   Starring. . . .

> *Shot of* FENTRY. *Standing, staring in space, expressionless.*

ANNOUNCER (VO)   Richard Boone

> *Shot of* SARAH. *Standing, busily sewing.*

ANNOUNCER (VO)   Kim Stanley

> *Shot of* ED PRUITT. *Attentively, smoking pipe.*

ANNOUNCER (VO)   Chill Wills

> *Shot of* MRS. HULIE. *In profile, then turns to left screen as if something needs her attention.*

ANNOUNCER (VO)   Beulah Bondi

> *Shot of* MRS. PRUITT. *Listening, with compassion, seated on porch.*

ANNOUNCER (VO)   Elizabeth Patterson

> *Shot of* PAPA FENTRY. *Standing and listening, with concern.*

ANNOUNCER (VO)   And guest star Charles Bickford.

The announcer introduces the show's sponsors: "Your Gas Company", Camel cigarettes, and All State Insurance Companies. Theme music comes to a dramatic close and revolving stars again appear on screen. The word "Tomorrow" appears over stars.

ANNOUNCER (VO)   On Playhouse 90. Act I of "Tomorrow." In just one minute.

Commercial break.

Music—a ballad-like harmonica and guitar theme used throughout the play—begins. Camera fades up on painted backdrop of tree, barn, and cottonfield. Screen credits fade in and out over the scene.

TOMORROW

Credit continues.

> Written by
> HORTON
> FOOTE

Credit continues.

> From a Short Story by
> WILLIAM
> FAULKNER

Camera begins to pan screen left.

> Directed by
> ROBERT
> MULLIGAN

Camera pans to porch where man and woman are sitting.

> Produced by
> HERBERT
> BRODKIN

Date appears on screen as pan comes to a stop.

> *1927*

EXTERIOR PRUITT HOUSE MORNING

The set is the front porch of a Mississippi farm house. It is a small, neat, well-built house. ED PRUITT, *fifty, sits on top of the porch stairs shelling peas. His mother, seventy, sits behind him in a rocking chair. Music fades out and the sputtering sound of a car motor fades up.* ED PRUITT *and* MRS. PRUITT *look to see who is coming.*

MRS. PRUITT   Whose car is that coming up the road?

PRUITT   I think it's . . . yeah . . . it's Lawyer Douglas's son's car.

MRS. PRUITT   What's he doing around here this time of morning?

PRUITT   Looks like he's coming to see us.

MRS. PRUITT   What's he want with us?

Motor sounds stop.

The opening scene of the television play featured veteran actors Chill Wills and Elizabeth Patterson along with younger cast members Charles Aidman and Jimmy Baird.

PRUITT   He probably is going to ask us some questions about Jackson Fentry.

MRS. PRUITT   Don't you tell him nothing, Pruitt.

PRUITT   Yes'm.

THORNTON DOUGLAS, *thirty, and his nephew,* CHARLES, *fourteen come up to the porch.*

THORNTON   Howdy.

PRUITT   Howdy, Thornton.

MRS. PRUITT   Morning.

THORNTON   How you been feeling, Mrs. Pruitt?

MRS. PRUITT   Pretty well.

THORNTON   You're looking very well.

MRS. PRUITT   Thank you, I can't complain.

THORNTON   This is my nephew, Charles. He's my partner, aren't you, boy?

CHARLES   Yes, sir.

PRUITT   Howdy, boy.

MRS. PRUITT   Sit down, son.

THORNTON *sits next to* PRUITT. CHARLES *takes a seat on the steps below.*

THORNTON   He likes riding out here in the country with me. *(pause)* I suppose you folks know I'm a lawyer now.

PRUITT   Yes, sir. We heard about it.

THORNTON   Well, I tried my first case yesterday, and I lost it. And I'm trying to figure out why. Seems a month ago Buck Thorpe ran off with H. T. Bookwright's daughter. Bookwright went after him; Thorpe pulled a gun and Bookwright killed him. Everybody knows Buck Thorpe was a wild bully, and if Bookwright hadn't killed him, someone else probably would have sooner or later. So, nobody figured a jury in this county would ever convict

Bookwright. Well, the jury didn't convict him, but they didn't free him either. There was one man that voted against freeing him and that hung the jury. The case is going to have to be retried next month. Do you know who the man was that hung my jury? *(pause)* Your neighbor, Jackson Fentry. And I just can't figure it out. Jackson Fentry was born and raised and lived all his life out here in the country, thirty miles from Frenchman's Bend where the killing took place. And he swore under oath he had never seen Bookwright before, and I could look at him and tell he never had enough time off from hard work to learn how to lie in.

He looks at them for some confirmation of his observation, but he gets none from them.

THORNTON   So I was just wondering if maybe you folks could tell me. . . .

PRUITT   *(Interrupting)* Nothing I can tell you, Thornton. You want to know anything about Jackson Fentry, you go to talk to him or his Pa. I expect you can find them home right now.

THORNTON   Yeah, I expect I can. Do you think they would tell me anything?

PRUITT   No, sir.

Camera pans toward DOUGLAS. MRS. PRUITT *listens attentively from behind.*

THORNTON   That's what I figured. *(pause)* Look, I don't mean any harm to anyone by coming out here today. It was just that this was my first case and it's very important to me to find out why I lost it—if I did something wrong in my presenting of it, or if no matter what I did, good or bad, Jackson Fentry would have still voted to convict Bookwright. If you choose to tell me, I'll never let it get by me to anyone else.

Camera pans left to include PRUITT *again.*

MRS. PRUITT   Pruitt. . . . Tell the boy what you know. He don't mean any harm to Jackson Fentry.

Theme music—a slow tempo strings—fades up.

PRUITT   Yes'm. Did you pass Jackson's farm coming out here?

THORNTON   Yes, sir.

PRUITT   It's poorer land even than it looks.

THORNTON   I expect so.

Camera moves in for tight shot of PRUITT.

PRUITT   But Jackson's Pa and Ma worked it. Made a living for themselves, paid their taxes, raised their family, and owed no man. I don't see how they done it, but they did.

DISSOLVE TO

EXTERIOR   FENTRY CABIN

It is twenty years earlier. Jackson Fentry is dishing out food from a pot on the wood stove. His father is at the table, eating. Jackson brings his food to the table and sits down. Neither he nor his father look at each other or exchange words.

PRUITT (VO)   And Jackson was helping from the time he was big enough to reach up to the plow handles. Until he was twenty-five and already looking forty, asking odds of nobody. Not married. Not nothing. Him and his Pa living alone and doing their own washing and cooking.

DISSOLVE TO

EXTERIOR   PRUITT HOUSE   NIGHT

PRUITT (VO)   One night about twenty-two or three years ago . . . in the summer of nineteen two, as well as I can remember, he came over here looking for me.

JACKSON FENTRY *approaches the porch. Music fades out as insect noises fade up.*

FENTRY   Pruitt. Pruitt.

MRS. PRUITT *comes to the door.*

MRS. PRUITT   Hello, Fentry.

FENTRY   Mrs. Pruitt, is your son at home?

MRS. PRUITT   No, he's gone into town. What do you want him for?

FENTRY   Well, I got me a job over at the sawmill at Frenchman's Bend. I traded a man to help my Daddy out while I'm gone. I wonder if you and your son would be kind enough to look in on him now and again and be sure he's all right while I'm gone.

MRS. PRUITT   I sure will.

FENTRY   Thank you.

MRS. PRUITT   How long are you going to be gone?

FENTRY   I don't know.

MRS. PRUITT   Good luck to you.

DISSOLVE TO

EXTERIOR   SAWMILL   MORNING

The sound of a whistling wind and theme music fades up. ISHAM QUICK, *twenty, the young son of the sawmill owner, comes around the corner of the boiler room.*

PRUITT (VO)   Jackson Fentry stayed at the sawmill two years. I remember he came home the first Christmas, visited with his Papa, and the next day he got up before daylight and walked back to that sawmill.

DISSOLVE TO

INTERIOR   BOILER ROOM

It is a small room, with a bed, a chair, and a barrel. There is a stove in one corner of the room for cooking. This is where FENTRY *now lives. It is just before Christmas of his second year at the sawmill. He is eating his breakfast as* ISHAM *enters.*

PRUITT (VO)   When the next Christmas come, we were expecting him home again . . .

ISHAM   Merry Christmas, Fentry.

FENTRY   Merry Christmas, Isham.

ISHAM   Pa wants to know if you're going home for Christmas again this year?

FENTRY   I am. I'm leaving soon as I can finish eating this.

ISHAM *warms his hands at the stove.*

ISHAM   How far is your farm?

FENTRY   Thirty miles.

ISHAM   How you get there?

FENTRY   I walk it.

ISHAM   When will you be back?

FENTRY   Day after Christmas.

ISHAM   Same as last year, huh? *(pause)* Don't you get lonesome all by yourself out here this way?

FENTRY   Nope.

Richard Boone, best known to TV audiences as the rugged star of Have Gun Will Travel, *played the part of the reticent hill farmer Jackson Fentry with sincerity; Andrew Prine portrayed Isham.*

ISHAM   Do you ever go hunting?

FENTRY   I hunt some.

ISHAM   Well, when you get back, maybe you and me can go hunting together sometimes.

FENTRY   All right.

ISHAM *stands for a moment watching* FENTRY *eat. He can think of nothing else to say and starts out the door.*

ISHAM   So long.

FENTRY   So long.

ISHAM *goes out the door.* FENTRY *finishes the little food he prepared for himself and goes out the door.*

CUT TO

EXTERIOR   SAW MILL

FENTRY *scrapes the dish out and begins to wash it at the well, when he hears a noise. It is the low moan of someone in pain. He stands listening for a moment; the sound comes again. He steps back and calls.*

FENTRY   Isham? Isham?

There is no answer to his call. The sound comes again and he walks toward it. He goes over to a stack of lumber inside an open shed. Lying against the logs is a young WOMAN, *blonde-haired, poorly dressed, thin and gaunt, her clothes thin and worn and no protection at all against the cold. If she were not so ill and starved-looking, she might be pretty. Even so, there is pride and dignity in her face. He goes over to her and gently raises her up.*

FENTRY   Lady. Lady.

She opens her eyes slowly.

SARAH   Where am I?

FENTRY   You're at Mr. Ben Quick's sawmill. I'm the watch-man out here in the winter time when the mill is shut down. I heard you when I came out of the boiler room

Fentry finds Sarah lying in a woodpile.

door. You sounded to me like you was in pain. Are you in pain?

The woman shakes her head weakly, "No."

FENTRY   How long have you been here?

SARAH   Oh, I don't know. I knowed I was walking down the road back yonder. I remember feeling dizzy, and I said to myself, I hope I don't faint, but I guess I did. *(pause)* What day is it?

FENTRY   Christmas Eve.

SARAH   Is it morning or afternoon?

FENTRY   It's the late morning.

SARAH   Oh, then I haven't been here too long. It was early in the morning on Christmas Eve when I started this way.

She tries to get up. FENTRY *takes her by the arm.*

FENTRY   Let me help you.

SARAH   Thank you. I reckon I'd better be getting on now.

FENTRY   Mind your head.

He helps her up, but she is still very weak.

SARAH   I'm sorry. I guess I'm just going to have to rest a little bit longer. I haven't quite gotten my strength back.

FENTRY *removes his jacket and places it over her shoulders.*

FENTRY   Well, Lady. Would you let me help you into the boiler room? You can rest there by the fire. It's raw and cold out here.

SARAH   Thank you. It has been a cold winter, hasn't it?

FENTRY   Yes, ma'am. It has.

SARAH   You know there was ice when I passed by the ditches this morning. I said to myself, Jack Frost has been here.

FENTRY   Yes, ma'am. He has.

Love comes to Fentry in the form of the lost and wandering Sarah, played with great emotional depth by Kim Stanley.

She gasps for breath. They pause for a moment.

FENTRY   Now, you just got to make it to that door there. Can you make it?

SARAH   Yes, sir. I can.

She rests again by the doorway for a moment.

SARAH   Thank you. You say it's nice and warm in here?

FENTRY   Oh, yes, ma'am.

CUT TO

INTERIOR   BOILER ROOM

Fentry helps her inside the door and to the chair. She sits slowly down and rests as if this little exertion was made at great cost.

FENTRY   Now you just come over here and sit right there and rest.

SARAH   Thank you. (*She looks around.*) It is nice and warm in here. I just love a good fire in the stove.

FENTRY   I was letting that one die out because I was just on my way to my Daddy's farm for Christmas. I could get it warmer.

SARAH   Oh, no, don't. Don't go to no trouble for me. I can't stay a minute. Just to get the cold out of my bones and some of my strength back.

A pause. She leans back against the chair. FENTRY *looks at her from behind.*

FENTRY   Can I get you anything to eat?

SARAH   No, thank you. You'd think I would be hungry, wouldn't you, carrying the baby this way, but I lost my appetite three months ago and I can't seem to get it back. I did used to love to eat too. (*She looks around.*) This where you live?

FENTRY   Yes, ma'am. Mr. Ben Quick is going to build me a

house in the spring, but he said in the meantime for me to live on out here. It's warm and dry and it does for me.

SARAH   I think it's fine. Have you been here long?

FENTRY   Over a year. Be two years in the spring.

SARAH   Is your home around here?

FENTRY   No, ma'am. I was raised on a cotton farm thirty miles from here that I worked with my Daddy. My Mama is dead; my Daddy is on that farm alone now. *(pause)* You from around here?

SARAH   Oh, sort of. On and off. My husband never did care much for this county. He was always trying to find work some place else. But we always had to come back.

FENTRY   You're on your way home now?

SARAH   No, sir.

FENTRY   Was you going into Jefferson?

SARAH   No, sir. I wasn't going no place. I was just going.

FENTRY   Just going? *(pause)* Is your husband dead?

SARAH   No, sir. My husband just disappeared when he found out about the baby coming. I stayed on with the people where we were living at the time, but last week two of their children got sick, and the husband was out of work, and I just figured it would be easier on them if I left, so I got up this morning while they were all asleep and just took off.

FENTRY   Don't you have any people?

SARAH   Oh, yes. I have a Papa and three brothers.

FENTRY   Can't you go on home to them?

SARAH   No, sir. You see they asked me to leave and never come back when I married my husband, and I don't ever intend to go back there.

FENTRY   But when they know . . .

SARAH   I don't intend to ever go back. My Papa has his pride; and I've got mine. *(pause)* You live here by yourself?

FENTRY   Yes ma'am.

SARAH   You're not a married man?

FENTRY   No, ma'am.

SARAH   I never did care very much for the winter time, did you?

FENTRY   No, ma'am. No, I didn't.

SARAH   You know, it seems like every winter I get sick. A woman come over the place I was staying and she said to me, "You look sick to me. You ought to see a doctor." I said, "Well, nothing wrong with me that a little sunshine wouldn't cure."

FENTRY   Would you like me to put some more wood on that fire?

SARAH   No, it's just fine. *(She rubs her hands.)* I do love the sunshine. I said to myself this morning when I left the house, I'm going, if my strength holds out, till I get to a place where it's warm and the sun is shining. *(pause)* Well, my strength didn't hold out very long, did it?

The wind whistles around the corners of the boiler room.

SARAH   Listen to that wind. Oh, I tell you that wind was cold walking into it the way I had to. It just cut right through you like a knife. It knew no mercy. *(She begins to tremble.)* Look at that, what's the matter with me? I just think about that wind and I start to tremble and shake. *(She closes her eyes.)* Look at that.

FENTRY   Lady. Why don't you come over here and rest on the bed? You can't rest good in a chair like that.

SARAH   No. I can't stay.

FENTRY   Just for a minute.

Theme music fades up slowly.

SARAH Well, all right. Just for a minute. *(She lies down on the bed.)* Oh, my, this does feel good. I don't believe you told me your name.

FENTRY Fentry. Jackson Fentry.

SARAH Fentry.

FENTRY And you're Mrs—?

Camera moves in for close-up of SARAH.

SARAH Eubanks. Sarah Eubanks. I was a Thorpe, but I married a Eubanks. You know, if I have a little girl, I'm going to name her Vesta after my Mama. If I have a boy, I think I'll . . . *(pause)* I don't know now. I was going to name him after my husband, but now I don't know . . .

The wind again howls around the boiler room.

SARAH You know, when I was a little girl of ten, my Mama died, and they say I got everything all mixed up that winter, because I grieved so. The wind would blow around my house, I would think it was my Mama calling to me and I would answer and call back to her and ask her where she was hiding. *(pause)* I never did grieve no more after that. After that, I vowed to myself that nothing would ever break my heart again, and it didn't, not for the longest kind of a time.

She has closed her eyes. She is soon asleep. FENTRY *watches her quietly from a chair by the stove. Music and wind noises fade out.*

Commercial break.

FADE OUT

Theme music up in lively tempo.

FADE IN

EXTERIOR SAWMILL NIGHT

Wind blows fiercely. FENTRY *quietly opens the boiler room door. Music fades out slowly.*

CUT TO

INTERIOR   BOILER ROOM

SARAH is still asleep on the bed. FENTRY *comes in and lights the kerosene lamp. He puts more wood in the stove. She wakes up as he is doing this.*

SARAH   Fentry?

FENTRY   Yes, ma'am.

SARAH   How long have I been asleep?

FENTRY   Ten hours.

SARAH   Ten hours?

FENTRY *turns around.*

FENTRY   Yes'm.

SARAH   Why didn't you wake me up?

FENTRY   Well, I figured the sleep would be good for you.

Sarah accepts Fentry's offer to stay with Fentry because, as she candidly admits, "I don't have the strength to go."

SARAH   My heavens.

FENTRY   You feel better?

SARAH   Well, yes, I do, but I'm ashamed and mortified. You ought to have waked me, or gone on off . . .

FENTRY   Well, I didn't have any place to go.

SARAH   Aren't you going to your farm for Christmas?

FENTRY   No ma'am.

SARAH   I thought you . . .

FENTRY   No, I changed my mind.

SARAH   What made you do that?

FENTRY   I just changed it.

SARAH   Is it still cold out yonder?

FENTRY   Yes, it is. Why don't you stay on here the rest of the night?

SARAH   Well. . . .

FENTRY   I can make a pallet for myself right here on the floor by the stove.

SARAH   Well, I wouldn't want to put you out any.

FENTRY   You wouldn't put me out any.

SARAH   Have you had your supper yet?

FENTRY   No ma'am.

SARAH   Can I fix it for you?

FENTRY   No'm, you stay on in bed.

SARAH   I want to do something.

FENTRY   I can get it.

FENTRY   While you were asleep I went to the store at Frenchman's Bend and I bought you this. (*He hands her a small sack.*) I thought you might like it.

SARAH   Thank you. *(She opens the sack.)* Well, I declare. It's hard candy.

FENTRY   Merry Christmas.

SARAH   Thank you. Merry Christmas to you, too.

FENTRY   If I fixed you something to eat now, would you eat it?

SARAH   No, thank you. I'm still not hungry. I'll just have a piece of my Christmas candy. *(She cries.)*

FENTRY   *(He stands.)* Lady, what are you crying for?

SARAH   I don't know. I'm just tired and nervous, I guess. I've been crying a lot lately. It don't mean nothing. I stop just as soon as I start. *(She wipes her eyes.)* You see. You know, I never used to cry at all. When I was a little girl, people used to accuse me of being hard-hearted, because nothing could get me to cry . . . I just say if that's the way it's got to be, that's the way it's got to be. . . . But lately that's all changed. Somebody'll come up to me and say good morning or good evening, and I'll cry, or ask me what time is it, and I'll just cry. Did you ever hear of anything like that? I didn't use to talk so much either. I used to be able to go a whole day without saying one single word. Lately, I can't stand it silent or quiet. *(pause)* You know what worries me most about death?

FENTRY   No'm.

SARAH   That it's silent in the grave. No one to talk to, no one to talk to you. *(She tastes a piece of candy.)* Oh, it's so good. *(She offers him the sack.)* Would you like some?

FENTRY   No, thank you.

SARAH   Who do you talk to out here when you get lonesome?

FENTRY   Nobody. There's nobody out here in the wintertime but me.

SARAH   Don't you miss having somebody to talk to?

FENTRY   Sometimes. *(pause)* Why don't you stay on here

until after your baby is born? I got food enough for the both of us. And it's warm here and dry.

SARAH Mr. Fentry . . . I . . .

FENTRY Well, you don't have to answer me right away. I'll get us some more wood for this fire and you think on it and when I come back you let me know what you decided.

He goes out. Theme music up slowly. She sits up in bed, eating a piece of candy. She looks around the boiler room. She gets up and tosses the covers tentatively across the bed. She reaches for the door handle. FENTRY comes in with the wood. The wind howls as he enters. He puts the wood down.

FENTRY It's even getting colder out than it has been.

He goes to the stove to warm his hands. She stands by the door.

SARAH Did you mean what you said about my staying on here?

FENTRY Yes ma'am.

SARAH Well, then I'll stay. Because to tell you the truth, I don't have the strength to go.

FENTRY *puts wood on the fire. Music fades out.*

FADE OUT

Commercial break.

Stars appear.

ANNOUNCER (VO) After station identification we shall continue with Act Two of "Tomorrow" on Playhouse 90.

Station identification.

FADE IN

Playhouse 90 theme music. Revolving stars appear. Playhouse 90 logo appears.

ANNOUNCER (VO)   Playhouse 90. Act Two of "Tomorrow."
Brought to you by the All State Insurance Companies.

FADE IN

Theme music up in lively tempo.

EXTERIOR   SAWMILL   DAY

A month later. FENTRY *is outside chopping wood.* SARAH
*comes out the door. Music slows and fades out as wind
sounds pick up.*

FENTRY   What are you doing out of the bed?

SARAH   Well, I feel better today. Oh, my. It's warmer today.

FENTRY   Yes, it is.

She comes out into the yard.

SARAH   You know something? I have been here for a month.

FENTRY *puts his axe down and goes to her.*

FENTRY   A month and three days. You ought to be back
inside. It's raw and cold out here.

SARAH   Well, I'll stay out a minute. The sun is so pretty.

FENTRY   Marry me, Sarah.

SARAH   I can't marry you. I've told you that. I got a husband
someplace.

FENTRY   He's deserted you.

SARAH   Well, I can't help that. He's still my husband in the
eyes of the law.

ISHAM QUICK *comes into the yard. He sees* SARAH. *He
seems surprised and embarrassed.*

ISHAM   Oh, pardon me. I didn't know you had company.

SARAH   Excuse me, I think I better go on in.

SARAH *goes inside the boiler room.*

ISHAM   Who's she?

FENTRY My wife.

ISHAM Since when? You didn't have her Christmas Eve when I was out here. You never mentioned you had a wife . . .

FENTRY She's my wife. Do you want us to leave?

ISHAM What do I want you to leave for? I don't care what you do out here. I didn't come here to spy. You can have twenty wives out here for all I care. I just come to get you to go hunting.

FENTRY Some other time.

ISHAM All right. (ISHAM *goes off screen and comes back in.*) Oh, Pa said to tell you to pick out the site of where you want your house. You and me can start building it this spring.

FENTRY I know where I want it.

ISHAM Well, maybe one day soon when it's warm I'll get him out here to look it over.

FENTRY All right.

ISHAM *leaves.* FENTRY *goes back to chopping wood.* SARAH *opens the door.* FENTRY *rushes to her.*

SARAH You'd better go get Mrs. Hulie. I think it's my time.

FENTRY Yes, ma'am, I will. Isham.

ISHAM Yeah?

ISHAM *comes back.*

FENTRY Isham, will you do me a favor?

ISHAM Sure.

FENTRY Will you go over and get Mrs. Hulie, the midwife, and tell her to come out here right away?

ISHAM Yeah, I'll be glad to.

FENTRY Thank you.

ISHAM *hurries off.* FENTRY *goes back into the boiler room.*

CUT TO:

INTERIOR   BOILER ROOM

FENTRY *helps* SARAH *into the bed.*

FENTRY   I got Isham to go for me.

SARAH   Who's he?

FENTRY   That young man who was just here. His Daddy owns the sawmill.

SARAH   Was he surprised to see me out here?

FENTRY   I reckon so.

SARAH   Did he ask who I was?

FENTRY   Yes, ma'am.

SARAH   What did you tell him?

FENTRY   I told him that you were my wife. *(She shivers.)* Are you cold again?

SARAH   Yes, I am, all of a sudden.

He goes to the stove and puts the wood in. He returns to the bedside.

FENTRY   Isham said his Daddy wanted me to pick out the place where I want the house to be. I said I already knew where I wanted it. And when you're stronger, I'll show you.

SARAH   I'd like to see that.

She has a sudden spasm of pain. She grabs his arm.

SARAH   I'm afraid.

FENTRY   You're afraid of what?

SARAH   I'm afraid I'm gonna die.

FENTRY   From childbirth? You're not going to die from that. Lots of women . . .

SARAH No, I'm not afraid of childbirth.

FENTRY Of what, then?

SARAH I don't know.

FENTRY You're going to get up from here feeling fine. Carrying this baby just wore you out . . .

She has another seizure of pain.

SARAH Oh, Fentry. *(He holds her.)* I ain't had much in my life, and that's the truth. Work and hunger and pain. I don't want to die. I don't want to die.

FENTRY You listen to me. You're not going to die. I am not going to let you die.

She relaxes and lies back on the bed.

FENTRY You hear me? You hear me? Now, you rest. You're going to need your strength when Mrs. Hulie gets here.

SARAH You don't leave me if I sleep.

FENTRY No ma'am.

SARAH In the summer time it's warm in the day and in the night. In the summer that ole sun just burns and cooks the pain and tiredness right out of you. Don't leave me.

FENTRY No ma'am. I'm not ever going to leave you unless you ask me to. Never. Never. Never.

She closes her eyes. He watches for a moment. He picks up the axe and goes back outside. We hear wind sounds and the sound of wood being chopped. SARAH *wakes up and sees that he's not there.*

SARAH *(Screaming)* Fentry! Fentry!

He comes running in to her with a bundle of firewood in his arms.

SARAH Don't leave me.

FENTRY I had to get this kindling wood. We'll need it when Mrs. Hulie gets here.

SARAH   Oh, of course. I'm sorry. I'm sorry. I'll be all right.

SARAH closes her eyes. FENTRY *goes outside. She has another spasm of pain, but doesn't call for him this time. She sits up and sings in a frail voice: "Oh, the moon shines tonight on the pretty red wing. The night birds calling. . . ."*

FADE OUT

Commercial break.

Music fades up.

FADE IN:

EXTERIOR   SAWMILL

FENTRY *stands by a pile of lumber. When* MRS. HULIE, *the midwife, a large, buxom woman, comes out of the boiler room, he turns immediately to her.* MRS. HULIE *goes to the well and washes her hands.*

Well-known character actress Beulah Bondi brought a more stern demeanor to the role of the midwife, Mrs. Hulie, than did her film counterpart Sudi Bond.

MRS. HULIE   The baby's here. A fine boy.

FENTRY   Thank you.

Music fades out.

MRS. HULIE   I'm worried about the Mama though. She isn't doing too well. I ain't going to lie to you, Mr. Fentry. I think she is in serious condition. She asked me straight out how she was, and I told her I didn't think she was doing too well, and she asked me to tell you that.

MRS. HULIE *folds up flour sacks. Wind howls.*

FENTRY   Yes, ma'am.

MRS. HULIE   She says she's afraid she's going to die and that she won't never get up off that bed in there. And I hate to tell you this, Mr. Fentry, but I don't think she will neither.

FENTRY   Was it having the baby?

MRS. HULIE   Oh, no. She was sick long before the baby. No, she just played out, it seems to me. She wants to see you now.

CUT TO

INTERIOR   BOILER ROOM

He goes over to her on the bed. He looks down at her. She has the baby beside her. The baby cries.

SARAH   It's small, ain't it?

FENTRY   Yes, it is.

SARAH   Not a bit pretty, is it?

FENTRY   New babies never are.

SARAH   How many new babies you seen in your life?

FENTRY   Not many.

SARAH   It's a boy.

FENTRY   That's what Mrs. Hulie said.

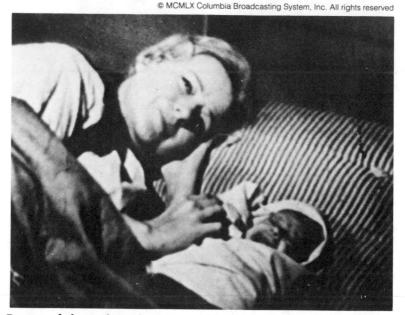

Pre-taped shots of Sarah with a real baby were inserted into the live action.

SARAH   So I don't guess, since it's a boy, it don't matter if it's pretty or not. He's light-complected, like me.

FENTRY   It's a fine-looking baby. Hello, son. Welcome. Can I hold the baby?

SARAH   Sure.

FENTRY *takes the baby in his arms.*

FENTRY   Well, now, he's small isn't he?

SARAH   Fentry. . . .

FENTRY   Yes ma'am.

SARAH   If anything does happen to me, will you take care of the baby?

FENTRY   Nothing is going to happen to you.

SARAH   If it does?

FENTRY   Well, if it would, then you could rest easy. I'll take care of this baby.

SARAH   Like he was your own?

FENTRY   Like he was my own.

SARAH   Thank you. Fentry . . .

FENTRY   Yes, ma'am.

SARAH   You know, when my husband left he told me I'd never see him again or find him again so not to try. And I been thinking, how can you divorce a man you can't find? And so, if you still want to marry me, I'm willing.

FENTRY   I want to marry you.

SARAH   You think you could find somebody to marry us right away?

FENTRY   Yes, ma'am. Preacher Whitehead's seven miles from here.

SARAH   Will you hurry?

FENTRY   Yes ma'am.

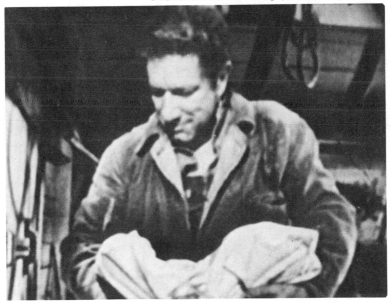

Boone did his best to convince the viewers that a real infant lay in his arms. In this scene, however, it is only swaddling clothes.

Intimate scenes like this made Boone and Stanley's performances moving and memorable.

FENTRY *hurries out the door.* MRS. HULIE *enters the boiler room. She dries flour sacks in front of stove.*

MRS. HULIE   You know, I've placed you. Weren't you a Thorpe? Didn't you have a Papa and three brothers and live with them on a farm back yonder?

SARAH   Yes ma'am.

MRS. HULIE   Don't you think they ought to be sent for at a time like this?

SARAH   I don't want them to know anything about me.

MRS. HULIE   I found these flour sacks over there I split in two for you. When Mr. Fentry comes back, I'll show him how they can be used for diapers.

MRS. HULIE *lays the sacks in crib.*

SARAH   All right.

MRS. HULIE *goes over to* SARAH.

MRS. HULIE   Now, let me have the baby. I'll put him in this box over here Mr. Fentry and me fixed up for a crib.

SARAH   Thank you.

Music—an eerie plucking sound—fades up.

MRS. HULIE   Now you try and get some sleep.

MRS. HULIE *takes the baby and puts him in a box in the corner of the room.*

SARAH   Mrs. Hulie? Is it cold in here Mrs. Hulie?

MRS. HULIE   No, honey. It's hot as everything. Now you try and sleep.

Music out. Wind noises up. SARAH *closes her eyes.*

DISSOLVE TO

EXTERIOR   SAWMILL

FENTRY *and* PREACHER WHITEHEAD *approach out of the dark and enter the boiler room.*

CUT TO

INTERIOR   BOILER ROOM

MRS. HULIE *is asleep in her chair.* FENTRY *and* PREACHER WHITEHEAD *come into the room.* WHITEHEAD *is in his fifties, a strong, kind man.* FENTRY *goes over to* SARAH'S *bed. He gathers her up in his arms.*

PREACHER WHITEHEAD   Hello, Mrs. Hulie.

MRS. HULIE *gets up.* PREACHER WHITEHEAD *warms himself by the stove.*

FENTRY   I got the Preacher here.

SARAH   That's fine.

The PREACHER *takes his Bible out of his pocket. He goes over to the edge of the bed.*

PREACHER   Hello, missus.

SARAH   Hello, Preacher.

MRS. HULIE *gets the lantern and brings it over and holds it by the* PREACHER.

PREACHER   "Dearly Beloved, we are gathered here together here in the sight of God and the face of this company to join together this man and this woman in holy matrimony. Do you, Jackson Fentry, take this woman to be your lawful wedded wife?"

FENTRY   I do.

PREACHER   Do you, missus? What's your name?

SARAH   Eubanks. Sarah Eubanks.

PREACHER   Sarah Eubanks, do you take this man to be your lawful wedded husband?

SARAH   Yes, I do.

PREACHER   Then I pronounce you man and wife. And may peace be with you in the name of the Father, and the Son, and the Holy Ghost. Amen.

Sarah and Rentry recite marriage vows moments before Sarah's death.

SARAH *lies down.* FENTRY *leans over her.*

SARAH   While you were gone, I had a terrible dream that I was freezing to death. I never seen snow and I don't know what it feels like or looks like, but in my dream I kept saying I'm drowning in the cold. I kept calling to you to save me.

FENTRY   And didn't I save you?

SARAH   I don't know. I want you to name the baby. You want to?

FENTRY   Thank you, I'd like to. While I was bringing the Preacher here, I went right by the place where our house is going to be. It's going to have three rooms in it—three rooms and a porch for us to sit on. And around it I'm going to put some pretty trees . . . a chinaberry tree and a hackberry tree and an oak tree.

SARAH   You think of a name for the baby yet?

FENTRY   No'm. I've been studying about it, but I haven't thought of one yet.

SARAH   Will you bring me the baby?

FENTRY   Yes'm. Are you all right?

SARAH   *(Weakly)* Yes. Please get my baby.

Music a slow guitar sound—fades up. FENTRY *goes over to the box and gets the baby. He comes back to* SARAH *and is about to give the baby to her when he looks down at her face. She is dead. He is not able yet to accept this.*

FENTRY   Sarah, I've got the baby here for you. Sarah, I got the baby here . . . *(Calling.)* Mrs. Hulie. Preacher.

MRS. HULIE *and the* PREACHER *come to the bedside of the woman.* MRS. HULIE *feels for her pulse.*

MRS. HULIE   She's dead.

FENTRY   No, ma'am. She's not dead. I'm not going to let her die. I'm going to save her.

MRS. HULIE   You can't save her now, Mr. Fentry. She's dead.

FENTRY doesn't protest any longer. He stands looking at SARAH. MRS. HULIE *takes the baby from him. She puts the baby back in the box and goes outside with the* PREACHER. FENTRY *stands looking at his wife. Music fades out.*

FENTRY   I don't know why we met when we did or why I found you when you was all wore out, and I couldn't save you no matter how bad I wanted to. I don't know why you want me to raise this baby instead of your folks. Or what they done to make you turn so against them; but I don't care. I promised you I'd raise him, and I will. Like he was my own.

Baby cries. FENTRY *goes over to the box and looks down at the baby.*

FENTRY   Son, your mama is dead. But I'm gonna raise you and see to you. I'll be your Papa and your Mama. And you'll never want or do without while I have breath left in my bones.

FENTRY *cries.*

FADE OUT.

Commercial break.

"Playhouse 90" theme music up. Revolving stars appear.

ANNOUNCER (VO)   Playhouse 90. Act Three of "Tomorrow" brought to you by Camel cigarettes . . .

Commercial break.

FADE IN

Theme music up in lively tempo.

EXTERIOR   FENTRY CABIN   DAY

FENTRY *and* ISHAM *drive into the yard in the buggy.* ISHAM *hitches the goat to a post.* FENTRY *carries the box with the baby to the front porch.* PAPA FENTRY *comes out on the porch.*

FENTRY   Hello, Papa. I'm home.

Music fades out.

PAPA   I see you are.

FENTRY   I'm home for good.

PAPA   I'm glad, son.

FENTRY   Papa, this is Isham Quick. His Daddy owned the sawmill where I was working.

ISHAM   Howdy, Mr. Fentry.

PAPA   Howdy. I was looking for you Christmas day, Fentry.

FENTRY   Yes, sir. But I couldn't get home Christmas day.

PAPA FENTRY *looks down at the baby.*

PAPA   Who does that belong to?

FENTRY   Me. It's my baby. I got married.

PAPA   Where's your wife?

FENTRY   She died.

PAPA   And is this your baby?

FENTRY   Yes, sir.

PAPA   Boy or girl?

FENTRY   Boy.

PAPA   What you name it?

FENTRY   Well, I thought I would name it after the two generals you served under. Jackson and Longstreet. If it's all right with you.

PAPA   That's fine with me.

PAPA FENTRY *takes the baby from his son.*

PAPA   Come here to me, Jackson and Longstreet Fentry.

ISHAM *gets in buggy.* FENTRY *turns to him.*

ISHAM   Well, you don't need me for nothing else, so I'll be going on back home.

FENTRY   I sure thank you.

ISHAM   That's all right. Good luck.

FENTRY   Good luck to you.

ISHAM *drives off.* FENTRY *goes back to porch.*

PAPA   Is he a good baby, boy?

FENTRY   Yes, sir. How you been, Papa?

PAPA   Pretty well.

FENTRY   How's that man I hired to help you been?

PAPA   He's all right. I guess this is the reason I didn't see you Christmas.

FENTRY   Yes, sir.

PAPA   I'm sorry I didn't get to meet your wife, son. What was her name?

FENTRY   Mary.

PAPA   What did she die of?

FENTRY   She jus' died. She was poorly when I met her.

FENTRY *and his father enter the Fentry cabin.*

CUT TO

INTERIOR   FENTRY CABIN

PAPA FENTRY *puts the baby crib on table.*

PAPA   None of us Fentrys have luck with their wives. Your Mama died when she warn't thirty. My Mama didn't live to see thirty-four. How old was your wife when she died, son?

FENTRY   Well, I don't know. I never asked her.

PAPA   He's small. I'd forgotten how small they was. How you going to feed him?

Papa Fentry, played by guest star Charles Bickford, accepts the conditions of his son's homecoming in a dignified and touching way.

FENTRY   I got that goat out there for his milk.

PAPA   You think we can raise him?

FENTRY   Yes, sir. I think we can.

PAPA   Well, if he's yourn, he's welcome. You better keep him in my room. I'll sleep in here.

FENTRY   Soon as he's big enough to come along, I'll start helping around the farm again. You still have that man I hired to help you?

FENTRY *folds diapers.*

PAPA   Yes, I do.

FENTRY   I asked the Pruitts to look in on you now and again. Did they do it?

PAPA   They have. Near about every day. One or t'other of them come snooping around. What you say your wife's name was, son?

FENTRY Sally . . .

PAPA That wasn't the name you said before.

FENTRY Wasn't it?

PAPA No, sir. I could have sworn before you said it was Mary.

FENTRY *walks toward his father.*

FENTRY Most likely I did. See, she had a kind of double name, Sally Mary. Sometimes I'd call her one and sometimes the other. But her name was Sally Mary.

PAPA Sally Mary what?

FENTRY Smith.

PAPA Did her people live up around Frenchman's Bend?

FENTRY No, sir, she come from the northern part of the state.

MRS. PRUITT *calls from outside.*

MRS. PRUITT Mr. Fentry.

PAPA That's Mrs. Pruitt. You want her to know you're here?

FENTRY I don't care, Papa.

PAPA FENTRY *goes to the door.*

PAPA Come in, Mrs. Pruitt.

She comes into the room.

MRS. PRUITT Hello, Jackson. Was that you come driving up in that buggy?

FENTRY Yes'm.

MRS. PRUITT Welcome home.

FENTRY Thank you.

MRS. PRUITT I see you have a new goat out in the yard, Mr. Fentry.

PAPA It's Jackson's. He brought it home with him from Frenchman's Bend to feed his baby.

MRS. PRUITT   His baby?

PAPA   He married him a wife while he was working up there at the sawmill. She died when the baby was born and he brung it home to raise.

MRS. PRUITT   Where is your baby, Jackson?

FENTRY   Yonder in the box.

MRS. PRUITT *goes over to the box and looks down at the baby.*

MRS. PRUITT   How old is the baby?

FENTRY   Three days.

MRS. PRUITT   What was the name of your wife, son?

FENTRY   Mary Sally Smith.

MRS. PRUITT   She come from around there?

FENTRY   No'm. She was from downstate.

MRS. PRUITT   So sorry to hear about it. Why, son, the baby doesn't have any clothes on.

FENTRY   Well no'm. I didn't have any for him. I'm going to have to make him some.

MRS. PRUITT   Have you got any diapers for him?

FENTRY   Mrs. Hulie, the midwife over in Frenchman's Bend, showed me how to tear these flour sacks in half and I been using them for diapers.

MRS. PRUITT   Well, I'll make some diapers for you and bring them over this evening.

FENTRY   Well, thank you. I don't want you to bother none.

MRS. PRUITT   It's no bother. If there is anything at all I can do, you just let me know?

FENTRY   Yes'm.

She starts out of the room. She pauses at the door and turns back into the room.

MRS. PRUITT   Son, why don't you just let me take the baby on home with me?

FENTRY   No, thank you . . .

MRS. PRUITT   At least until it can be weaned.

FENTRY   No, thank you. I wouldn't care to do that.

MRS. PRUITT   You can stay at my house, too, if you want to.

FENTRY   Thank you very much. But I can make out.

MRS. PRUITT   Well, all right. Call me if you change your mind.

PAPA   We will, Mrs. Pruitt.

She goes out. PAPA FENTRY *goes to his son's baby.*

PAPA   Son, you'd better get your wife's name straight. You told me it was Sally Mary Smith. You told Mrs. Pruitt it was Mary Sally Smith.

FENTRY   Well. . . .

PAPA   Which one was it? *(A pause.)*

FENTRY   It wasn't neither. It was Sarah Eubanks. And she was from around Frenchman's Bend, but where exactly, I don't know.

PAPA   Well, why do you want to keep this a secret?

FENTRY   I'm not this baby's papa. I met his mother after his father had deserted her. She was sick; I took her into my house; cared for her. After this baby was born, we were married. I promised her I would raise this baby as if it were my own. And I will, too.

PAPA   Well, that's fine, but what if this baby's papa or your wife's people find out about it? Supposing they come here and try to take him away from you?

FENTRY   Well, that's never going to happen, Papa, because I'm never going to leave him or let him leave me until he's grown. Nobody's going to take him away from me. Nobody.

FENTRY *takes the baby to the bedroom and sets the box down on the bed. He tries to quiet the baby.*

FENTRY   Jackson and Longstreet. Oooo . . . son.

FADE OUT

Theme music up.

PRUITT (VO)   And Jackson Fentry raised that boy. I don't know how he was at sawmilling . . .

FADE IN

EXTERIOR   FENTRY CABIN

PAPA FENTRY *comes out on the front porch and ties his shoe.* FENTRY *and a small boy come out on the porch. The boy raises some suspenders over his shoulder. Music fades out.*

PRUITT (VO)   . . . and he never had enough of a farm to find out if he was any good at farming, but he raised that boy

Three generations of Southern manhood sit together on the Fentry front porch.

all by himself . . . When he was old enough, he took him into the fields with him . . .

FENTRY   Can you get those up by yourself? Come on, I'll help you. There now.

FENTRY *holds the boy in his lap.*

FENTRY   Look's like it's going to be a fine morning. Boy of mine going to be three years old tomorrow. Aren't you, boy?

JACKSON AND LONGSTREET   Yes, sir.

MRS. PRUITT *comes up.* FENTRY *stands with the boy in his arm.*

MRS. PRUITT   Good morning. How you all this morning?

FENTRY   Pretty fair.

MRS. PRUITT   How you, Jackson and Longstreet?

FENTRY   She's our neighbor. Say hello.

JACKSON AND LONGSTREET   Hello.

MRS. PRUITT   Now, I hope you're not going to mind what I been doing, but I had a little spare time and I had some cloth I didn't need. So I thought I'd make some clothes for your little boy.

FENTRY   Well, thank you.

MRS. PRUITT   I hope you don't mind my interfering, but I know how much you have to do without making his . . .

FENTRY   Well, I don't mind that, ma'am. Thank you for your trouble, and we'll be getting on to work.

FENTRY *and the boy leave.* PAPA FENTRY *comes up to* MRS. PRUITT.

PAPA   I hope he didn't hurt your feelings none.

MRS. PRUITT   No.

PAPA   He wants to do everything for that boy himself. Sometimes I think he begrudges the earth itself for what the boy has to eat to keep alive.

MRS. PRUITT   Oh, I don't mind. I'm not sensitive.

PAPA FENTRY *walks off.* MRS. PRUITT *looks around.*

MRS. PRUITT   Well, I guess I'd better be getting on home and get to my own work.

She leaves.

DISSOLVE TO

EXTERIOR   SAWMILL   DAY

Crows caw. Black men are working in the yard. ISHAM QUICK *comes out of the boiler room. The* SHERIFF *and the three* THORPE BROTHERS *come by.*

SHERIFF   Howdy.

ISHAM   Howdy.

SHERIFF   I'm the Sheriff. . . .

ISHAM   Howdy.

SHERIFF   These three men are the kin of Sarah Eubanks. We've been told that you could give us some information.

ISHAM   Oh, well, she died near three years ago. Right in yonder . . . (*He points to the boiler room.*) You'll find her grave back yonder in the woods. I put up a little wooden marker on the grave myself. . . .

LES THORPE   Well, thank you. We're her brothers. I'm Les. This is Bud, T.R.

ISHAM   Howdy do. I am Isham Quick.

LES THORPE   We've been told my sister gave birth to a child out here.

ISHAM   She did.

LES THORPE   Do you know where the baby is?

ISHAM   He's with his Daddy.

LES THORPE   No, he ain't. His Daddy is Leroy Eubanks. He deserted my sister before the child was born.

BUD THORPE   We've taken care of him.

LES THORPE   We only found all this out two days ago.

ISHAM   Well, I don't know anything about that, but I do know right in yonder she married Jackson Fentry, and there was witnesses to prove it. Brother Whitehead, the Preacher . . .

LES THORPE   *(Interrupting)* I don't care how many witnesses you have. She had a husband, a legal husband, so that marriage don't count for nothing. We want our own flesh and blood to raise ourselves.

ISHAM   But you wouldn't take that boy away from him. He taken that boy as his own when nobody come to claim him. He raised that boy, clothed and fed him for three years.

LES THORPE   We aim to do right about that, too, when we have seen the boy.

ISHAM   Mister, you can't walk up after three years. . . .

LES THORPE   He's our kin. We want him and we aim to have him. We'll pay this man for his trouble and for what the boy cost him. . . .

ISHAM   Well, you'll have to find them first. I don't know where they've gone to. They just disappeared one day after your sister died.

LES THORPE   We were told at the store that you drove them away . . . in a buggy. Him and the baby and a nanny goat.

ISHAM   Well, I don't know why anybody want to . . .

SHERIFF   You might as well tell us, if you know where they are. These men have been given the baby by its father. We'll find them if it takes a day or a month or a week. These men have the law on their side.

ISHAM   Yes, sir. Come on then. I'll take you to them. He lives on a farm about thirty miles from here.

LES THORPE   We're much obliged.

They start out.

DISSOLVE TO

EXTERIOR FENTRY CABIN DAY

FENTRY *has the boy in his arms.*

FENTRY   Look up there. Way, way up there. You know what that it? That's a chicken hawk. And you know what a chicken hawk does? A chicken hawk'll catch and kill your chickens if you got any. When you're bigger, I'm going to get you a gun, and you and me will go hunting chicken hawks together.

Hoofbeats signal the approach of the THORPE BROTHERS. FENTRY *puts the boy down. He is about to go back to chopping his wood when* ISHAM *comes into the yard. The boy sees him when* FENTRY *does. The boy clings to* FEN-TRY'S *leg.* FENTRY *holds the boy close to him as they approach.* ISHAM *goes forward to him.*

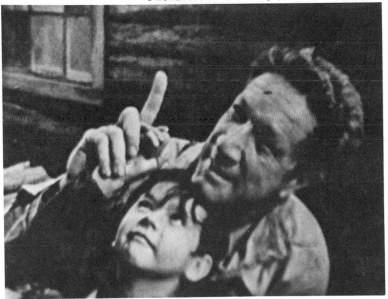

A child's presence on camera no doubt added some precarious mo-ments to the already high-pressured medium of live television. Boone keeps young actor Peter Oliphant tightly in hand in this scene.

ISHAM   Howdy, Fentry.

FENTRY   Howdy.

ISHAM   You remember me?

FENTRY   Yes, I do.

ISHAM   How you been?

FENTRY   Pretty fair. How you been?

ISHAM   That your boy there? That Jackson and Longstreet?

FENTRY   Say hello to Mr. Isham, son.

> *The boy hides behind* FENTRY. *He doesn't answer.*

ISHAM   Hey, boy.

> *The three* THORPE BROTHERS *approach.*

ISHAM   These here are your wife's brothers. These are the Thorpe boys.

FENTRY   Howdy.

THORPE BROTHERS   Howdy.

> FENTRY *studies them for a moment.*

FENTRY   What can I do for you?

LES THORPE   We've come for the boy.

FENTRY   What boy?

LES THORPE   That boy.

FENTRY   You can't have him. He's my boy.

LES THORPE   We're going to have him.

FENTRY   Run, son. Run to your granddad out in the fields.

> FENTRY *pushes the boy aside. He takes the axe and starts for the nearest* THORPE. ISHAM *sees what he is about to do and grabs the axe as a* THORPE *grabs* FENTRY. FENTRY *begins a terrible struggle as all three men try to hold him down.*

The Thorpe brother, outnumbering Fentry by three rather than the two Faulkner had described, subdue Fentry and take the boy away.

LES THORPE   Bud, catch the boy and take him to the surrey.

> BUD *pounces on* JACKSON AND LONGSTREET, *who kicks and fights but is taken off.* FENTRY *jerks and fights until the boy is out of sight. Then he gives a terrible cry of pain and collapses.* T.R. *and* LES THORPE *put him down on the porch steps. He slumps down.* ISHAM *stands behind them.*

FENTRY   I know it. I know'd it all along. I reckon that's why it taken me so by surprise. (*A pause.*) I'm all right now.

Hoofbeats signal departure of the group.

FADE OUT

Commercial break.

FADE IN

EXTERIOR   FENTRY CABIN   NIGHT

Music up.

PRUITT (VO)   Fentry left his farm the day the Thorpe boys

took Jackson and Longstreet away. Fentry was gone five years and if his Daddy knew where he was he sure wouldn't tell us.

Music out.

DISSOLVE TO

INTERIOR   FENTRY CABIN

PAPA FENTRY *is at the table eating.* FENTRY *comes through the door.*

FENTRY   Hello, Papa.

PAPA   Fentry . . .

FENTRY   How have you been?

PAPA   Pretty well. How have you been?

FENTRY   Pretty fair.

PAPA   You hungry? Beans on the stove.

FENTRY   Thank you.

> FENTRY *puts down his bundle and gets some food.*

PAPA   Where did you go, Fentry?

FENTRY   I did some cotton in Texas, some sugar fields in Louisiana. I don't know where all.

PAPA   Son, I've seen Jackson and Longstreet. I was over at Frenchman's Bend last month. I heard where he was living at. He's living on a cotton farm with his uncles. I rode my mule over there when I heard and I seen him. I passed him on the road. I knowed it was him. His hair was just as black and shiny. I said: "Hi, there, Jackson and Longstreet. Remember me?" "No, sir," he said, "and my name ain't Jackson and Longstreet," he says. "It's Thorpe. Buck Thorpe." (*A pause.*) He's eight years old now, son, and a fine looking boy, but he didn't have no notion as to who I was.

FENTRY *goes out quickly.*

CUT TO

EXTERIOR   FENTRY CABIN

ED PRUITT *comes by and calls to* FENTRY.

PRUITT   Hey, Fentry. We seen you coming home. Where all you been?

FENTRY   Texas. I don't know where all. . . .

PRUITT   Fentry . . .

FENTRY   Yes, sir.

PRUITT   What happened to him?

FENTRY   What happened to who?

PRUITT   The boy. Your Papa never'd tell us. Did he die?

FENTRY   What boy?

Guitar strikes a sudden chord. Camera freezes on close-up of Fentry.

DISSOLVE TO

FIELDS   FENTRY FARM   DAY

PAPA FENTRY *works the fields.* JACKSON FENTRY *is working alongside him. Music up.*

PRUITT (VO)   Well, sir, twelve years passed, and if they ever mentioned the boy again, we never heard of it.

Music out. PRUITT *comes into the field.*

PRUITT   Hey, you folks working your ground already? Mine's still too cold. Guess where I was yesterday, Fentry? Up at Frenchman's Bend. I passed that old sawmill you used to work in. They have been having a heap of excitement up that way.

FENTRY   That so?

PRUITT   A young bully named Buck Thorpe showed up. He must be a terror the way folks talk. Fights, drinks, and raises all kinds of Cain.

PAPA   What was his name?

PRUITT   Buck Thorpe. He must be a terror the way they tell it. Say, can one of ya'll come over to my place and give me a hand half a day tomorrow or the next?

FENTRY   I can.

PRUITT   Sure thank you. What day you want to come?

FENTRY   I'll be along tomorrow.

PRUITT   Much obliged. I'll be expecting you.

> PRUITT *goes.* FENTRY *stops working. Music fades up.*

FENTRY   I'm going over to Frenchman's Bend.

PAPA   Why, son?

FENTRY   I just have to look at him.

> FENTRY *goes.* PAPA FENTRY *goes back to work. Music out.*

> > DISSOLVE TO

FRONT OF A COUNTRY STORE   NIGHT

A crowd of men are watching Buck Thorpe scuffle with another man.

BUCK   Yell Calf Rope. Yell Calf Rope.

MAN   *(Weakly)* Calf Rope.

> BUCK THORPE *pushes him aside. He looks around at the other men standing on the porch. He takes a bottle of whiskey and has a swig.* FENTRY *comes in and stands watching.*

BUCK   *(To men)* I can lick anybody around here. Who wants to challenge me on that? *(He grabs a man.)* You want to challenge that?

MAN   Not me, Buck. I'm a friend of yours.

BUCK   How about you, Lee?

LEE   No, sir, Buck. No, sir.

BUCK *throws him aside.*

MAN Simmer down, man. We're friends.

The men sneak away. BUCK *sees* FENTRY *and yells at him.*

BUCK What do you want? What are you staring at me for? Huh? Go on, you. Get out of here. Get out of here.

FENTRY *walks away.* BUCK *watches him go. One of the men comes back.*

MAN Who is that old man, Buck?

BUCK Shoot, I don't know. I never seen him before.

BUCK *takes a swig of whiskey.*

PRUITT (VO) And so, a couple of days later, Bookwright killed Buck Thorpe. Of course, I never could associate all those names.

DISSOLVE TO

PRUITT'S PORCH

MRS. PRUITT, THORNTON, *and* CHARLES *are still sitting listening to* PRUITT. *Birds sing.*

PRUITT Thorpe meant nothing to me. But I ran into Isham Quick the day Fentry hung your jury, and he straightened it all out for me. Of course, he wasn't going to vote Bookwright free. . . .

THORNTON Of course, he wasn't. . . .

CHARLES I would have. I would have freed him. Because Buck Thorpe was bad.

THORNTON No, you wouldn't, son. (*He puts his hand on the boy's shoulder.*) No, it wasn't Buck Thorpe, the adult, the man. Jackson Fentry would have shot that man just as quick as Bookwright did if he had been in Bookwright's place. No. It was because somewhere in the debased and brutalized flesh which Bookwright slew there still remained, not the spirit, maybe, but at least the memory of that little boy, that Jackson and Longstreet Fentry, even though the man the boy became didn't know it, and only Fentry did. And you wouldn't have freed him either. Don't you ever forget that. Never.

THORNTON *looks across the fields toward the Fentry farm. Music up.*

DISSOLVE TO

FIELDS   FENTRY FARM

FENTRY *is working in the fields. He looks up for a moment, then goes back to work.*

THORNTON (VO)   The lowly and invincible of the earth—to endure and endure and then endure, tomorrow and tomorrow and tomorrow. Of course, he wasn't going to vote Bookwright free.

Camera holds on FENTRY *with cotton sack over his shoulder. Music fades out.*

FADE OUT

III
THE FILM

TOMORROW

Horton Foote

Lawyer Douglas, portrayed by Peter Masterson, makes a plea to the jury, composed primarily on local non-actors.

THE SCRIPT for the film *Tomorrow* printed here is a scene-by-scene transcription of the feature film released in 1972.

FADE IN

Car headlights approach out of the darkness as voice-over begins.

LAWYER DOUGLAS (VO)   Your honor, gentlemen of the jury, all of us in this country, the South, have been taught from birth a few things which we hold above all else.

EXTERIOR   H. T. BOOKWRIGHT'S HOUSE

Under cover of darkness BUCK THORPE *and* H. T. BOOK-WRIGHT'S *daughter embrace and sneak toward a 1920s era automobile.* THORPE *takes the daughter's suitcase; their evident haste and secrecy suggest an elopement.* BOOKWRIGHT, *shotgun in hand, comes out on the porch of his solidly-built frame house.* THORPE *pulls a gun on* BOOKWRIGHT *as voice-over continues.*

LAWYER DOUGLAS (VO)   One of the first of these is that only a life can pay for the life it takes.

BOOKWRIGHT *shoots* THORPE; THORPE *collapses.*

CUT TO

EXTERIOR   COURTHOUSE

Freeze-frame on a wide shot of the courthouse as the following screen credits appear.

A FILMGROUP PRODUCTION
TOMORROW

starring
ROBERT DUVALL

co-starring
OLGA BELLIN

with
SUDIE BOND
RICHARD MCCONNELL
PETER MASTERSON
JAMES FRANKS
WILLIAM HAWLEY
JOHNNY MASK

Voice-over continues and the scene comes to life outside the courthouse with the movement of a wagon and townspeople.

LAWYER DOUGLAS (VO)   Now I know there's not a man on this jury, or a man in Mississippi, that in his heart can find my client, Bookwright, guilty for defending his daughter against a rascal like Buck Thorpe.

CUT TO

INTERIOR   SMALL COUNTY COURTROOM

There are thirty or so people in the room including: H. T. BOOKWRIGHT, *a well-to-do middle-aged farmer who is being tried for murder; Bookwright's wife and daughter,* THE JUDGE, *the* DEFENSE ATTORNEY, *the* ASSISTANT DISTRICT ATTORNEY, THORNTON DOUGLAS; SPECTATORS *and* JURORS. *There is a sleepy atmosphere in the courtroom as* LAWYER DOUGLAS *addresses the jury. A Confederate flag hangs prominently behind him.*

LAWYER DOUGLAS   And that's what I'm talking about. Not about the dead man and his character or the morality of the act he was engaged in. Not about self-defense, whether or not this defendant was justified to the point of taking life, but about all of us, who are not dead. Human beings who at bottom want to do right.

Camera pans across the JURORS *until it comes to the last juror,* JACKSON FENTRY, *a dirt farmer, with a thin, wizened ageless face.*

LAWYER DOUGLAS   Human beings with all the complexities of human passions, instincts, beliefs. Thank you gentlemen. Thank you, Your Honor.

JUDGE   Court recessed until jury returns.

INTERIOR   JURORS' ROOM

The JURORS *are lounging in chairs, one stands by the window. The* FOREMAN *turns and approaches* FENTRY *who is sitting passively in a chair in a corner of the room.*

FOREMAN   Don't you agree he had a pistol in his hand when they found him?

Voices of JURORS *are heard in the background.*

1ST JUROR   Buck Thorpe deserved what he got.

2ND JUROR   I wouldn't have waited as long as Bookwright did.

FOREMAN *picks up a cup of coffee and paces the room.*

FOREMAN   He was not only no good but dangerous.

3RD JUROR   Right. Right.

FOREMAN   And if it hadn't been Bookwright, someone sooner or later would have to kill him.

FENTRY   Yes, sir.

FOREMAN   Then what do you want? What do you want?

FENTRY *stares solemnly at the floor.*

FENTRY   I can't help it. I ain't going to vote Bookwright free.

The Camera holds on FENTRY'S *silent face as* LAWYER DOUGLAS *begins his role as voice-over narrator.*

LAWYER DOUGLAS (VO)   And so, Jackson Fentry, cotton farmer, hung my jury. Who was he? I thought he'd farmed one place all his life. But I discovered that twenty years ago he left for a job.

DISSOLVE TO

A close-up of JACKSON FENTRY *as a clean-shaven young man.*

LAWYER DOUGLAS (VO)   His neighbors told me. You see, that was my first case and I had to find out why I lost it.

DISSOLVE TO

EXTERIOR   COUNTRY ROAD

FENTRY, *now a young man, walks down a country road. As he passes by a modest frame house, a neighbor waves to him.*

NEIGHBOR   Good luck to you, Fentry.

FENTRY *continues walking.*

LAWYER DOUGLAS (VO)   If any of us had known then what I know now, Jackson Fentry never'd been on that jury.

FENTRY *walks down the dirt road toward the camera. Music picks up; we hear voices of a church congregation in the rural South. The hymn, sung in a moderate tempo, is "Angels Rock Me to Sleep." Screen credits appear as follows.*

Production Manager	STEVEN SKLOOT
Asst. Director	ALAN HOPKINS
Asst. Unit Manager	MICHAEL HALEY
Script Supervisors	LILLIAN MACNEIL
	PAULA ROIZMAN
Art Director	BARBARA TINDALL

FENTRY *in full view, his coat over his shoulder. Close-up of his well-worn boots as he walks down dirt road.*

Tomorrow copyright MCMLXXI by
FILMGROUP PRODUCTIONS

Music picks up in volume and tempo. Piano accompanies. The predominant voice is that of a gravel-voiced older man.

Film group Productions

Fentry makes the thirty-mile walk to Frenchman's Bend. The decision to shoot on location in northeast Mississippi and to cast local persons as extras established a feeling of authenticity to the film.

Wardrobe	ED BREHNAN
Hair Stylist	BILL FARLEY
Property Master	FRED WEILER
Chief Carpenter	CARLOS QUILLES
Special Props	NOSTALGIA ALLEY, N.Y.

FENTRY *passes in front of a country store where several men are gathered on the porch. He nods but doesn't stop to speak.*

Camera Operator	GEORGE BOVILLET
Asst. Cameramen	JACK BROWN
	JOHN CONNOR
Sound	DAVID BLUMGART
Boom	JOSEPH SLIFKIN

Shot from behind of FENTRY *walking down road, then a shot of him from across a field. Dog barking in the background.*

Gaffer	TOM GESTARE
Grip	ED ENGELS, JR.
Assistant Gaffer	HARVEY SNOW
Assistant Grips	JIMMY BATTLE
	DEAN OLIVE
Casting	ELLEN ANTHONY
Production Sec.	RUTH DORIZZI
Special Asst. to the Producers	CHARLES CARMELLO
Production Assts.	JOHN AVERY
	MICHAEL COOKE
	JIMMY ROBBINS
	JAMES WYGUL

FENTRY *turns away from the road and walks into a yard.*

Assts. to the Editor	JULIE ZALE
	NANCY COOK
Sound Editing and Effects	JESS SORACI
	FILMSOUNDS, INC.
Sound Engineer	RICHARD VORISEK
Titles and Opticals	CINEFFECTS, INC.

EXTERIOR   SAWMILL

Music fades out. FENTRY *approaches a rough-looking log house. A young man comes out on the front porch and greets* FENTRY.

ISHAM   Hello.

FENTRY *nods.* ISHAM *walks down the porch steps.*

ISHAM   Can I help you?

FENTRY   I'm looking for Mr. Chet Russell.

ISHAM   Well, he's not here right now. I'm his son, Isham. (*pause*) You the man my father hired as caretaker?

FENTRY   Yes, sir.

ISHAM   Come on then.

FENTRY *follows* ISHAM *around the house and across a wooded yard. Half-finished timber lying on the ground shows evidence that the place is a sawmill.* ISHAM *points to a wooden shed and a pile of lumber, then leads* FENTRY *up a bank to another wood building.*

ISHAM   Last man we had left a month ago. Got too lonely for him. He was drunk half the time anyway. This is the sawmill. The men don't come out here till spring. Pa says you can stay on in the boiler room. He'll leave the mule out here so you can get to the store and back. Next year, if you still like it out here, we'll talk about building you a house.

INTERIOR   BOILER ROOM

A small disheveled room with very rustic furniture. The room also houses a large boiler and a small wood stove. ISHAM *leans in the doorway as* FENTRY *tentatively inspects the room.*

ISHAM   There's a stove there you can cook on. There's a well out there for water. We'll get you some dishes. If you need anything else, you come to the house and ask for me or Pa.

FENTRY   Yes, sir.

A montage of shots in and around the boiler room shows FENTRY'S *daily life of quiet industry and solitude. We see that he has brought a certain order to the squalor of his existence. Music of concertina and guitar picks up moderate tempo as screen credits continue. This theme, reminiscent of American folk tunes, is used throughout the film.*

Film Editor
REVA SCHLESINGER

FENTRY *comes out of the boiler room and takes a drink from the pump. He squats and peers out at the woods and empty dirt road. Inside the boiler room,* FENTRY *sharpens a knife. He begins to shave.*

The set for this interior scene, Fentry's boiler room, was constructed with the assistance of local townspeople, in the Tupelo, Mississippi, fairgrounds building.

Director of Photography
ALAN GREEN

Outside the boiler room, FENTRY *washes out clothes in a large tub. He wrings the clothes out and hangs them on a line.*

Music by
IRWIN STAHL

"Angels Rock Me to Sleep"
Sung by
THE JACKSON CAMP SINGERS

FENTRY *whittles inside the boiler room.*

Screenplay by
HORTON FOOTE

Based on the play, "Tomorrow," by HOR-TON FOOTE

Adapted from a story by WILLIAM
FAULKNER

FENTRY *sits with his back up against a tree. Inside the*
boiler room, he sews his clothing.

Produced by
GILBERT PEARLMAN
and PAUL ROEBLING

FENTRY *asleep on his cot in the boiler room.*

Directed by
JOSEPH ANTHONY

DISSOLVE TO

INTERIOR BOILER ROOM MORNING

FENTRY *is sitting at a table eating.* ISHAM RUSSELL *comes*
into the boiler room.

ISHAM Hey, Merry Christmas, Fentry.

FENTRY Merry Christmas, Isham.

ISHAM Pa wanted to know if you'd be going home for Christmas.

FENTRY I am. I'm leaving soon as I can eat this.

ISHAM How far is your farm?

FENTRY Thirty miles.

ISHAM How you gonna get there?

FENTRY I walk it. I'll be home before suppertime.

FENTRY *offers* ISHAM *a cup.*

FENTRY You want some?

ISHAM Thank you. When will you be back?

ISHAM *takes a cup of coffee off the stove and refills* FEN-
TRY'S *cup.*

FENTRY Day after Christmas.

ISHAM   Don't you ever get lonesome by yourself out here this way?

FENTRY   Nope.

ISHAM   You ever go hunting?

FENTRY   I hunt some.

ISHAM   Maybe when you come back, we can go hunting together sometime.

FENTRY   All right.

> ISHAM *stands for a moment watching* FENTRY. *Then, he sets down the cup.*

ISHAM   Thank you.

> FENTRY *nods.* ISHAM *goes out the door.*

EXTERIOR   YARD

> FENTRY *has finished the food he prepared for himself. He scrapes the dish and begins to wash it when he hears a noise. It is the low moan of someone in pain. He stands listening for a moment and the sound comes again.* FENTRY *walks over to a stack of lumber inside an open shed. Lying against the logs is a young woman, light-haired, gaunt, dressed in worn clothing that can barely protect her against the cold. If she were not so ill, she might be pretty.* FENTRY *bends down and gently rolls her over on her back. We now see that she is pregnant.* FENTRY *watches her for a moment and then gently tries to rouse her.*

FENTRY   Lady. Aw, Lady. Lady.

> *At first,* FENTRY *gets no response. The woman opens her eyes slowly. The sight of* FENTRY *frightens her. She hurriedly tries to get up but can't.*

SARAH   Where am I?

FENTRY   You're at Chet Russell's sawmill in Frenchman's Bend.

> FENTRY *looks down at the woman's thin, worn face.*

Fentry finds Sarah in the woodpile outside his cabin door.

FENTRY I'm Jackson Fentry. I'm the watchman out here in the wintertime when the mill is shut down. I heard you when I come out the door of the boiler room. You sounded to me like you was in pain.

The woman shakes her head weakly.

FENTRY How long you been here?

SARAH I don't know. I remember walking down the hill back yonder. I knowed I was feeling dizzy and I said to myself I hope I ain't going to faint, but I guess I did. What day is it?

FENTRY The morning before Christmas.

SARAH Then I haven't been here too long. It wasn't light yet when I started out this way.

SARAH *tries to get up.*

SARAH I think I'd better be getting on now.

FENTRY   Let me help you.

> FENTRY *helps her up, but she is still very weak and has to lean against a rough pole to keep from collapsing.*

SARAH   I'm sorry. I guess I will have to rest awhile longer. I haven't quite gotten my strength back yet.

FENTRY   Let me help you in here so you can rest by my fire. It's so raw and cold out here.

SARAH   It has been a cold winter, hasn't it?

FENTRY   Yes'm.

SARAH   There was ice this morning early when I left the house. I seen it on the ditches as I passed.

FENTRY   Yes'm.

SARAH   I said to myself Jack Frost has been here.

FENTRY   He sure had.

> SARAH *is gasping for breath; they pause for a moment.*

FENTRY   Can you make it?

> FENTRY *helps her inside the door.*

INTERIOR   BOILER ROOM

> FENTRY *helps* SARAH *over to a chair in front of the wood stove.*

FENTRY   You sit here, Mrs.

SARAH   Thank you.

> *Slowly,* SARAH *sits down on a chair and rests her head back against it.* FENTRY *stands beside her.*

SARAH   It is nice and warm in here. I love a good fire in the stove.

> FENTRY *goes to the stove and starts to feed it wood.*

FENTRY   I could get it warmer. I was letting it die out because I was about to leave for my Papa's farm for Christmas.

SARAH   Don't go to no trouble for me. I can't stay for more than a minute, just to get my strength back and to get some of the coldness out of my bones.

SARAH *leans in toward the fire.* FENTRY *closes the door. He dips a cloth in a pail of water and brings it to her.*

SARAH   Thank you.

FENTRY   Can I get you anything to eat?

SARAH   No, thank you. *(pause)* You'd think I'd be hungry wouldn't you carrying a baby and all but I don't have no appetite. You live here all by yourself?

FENTRY   Yes ma'm. Mr. Chet Russell is going to build me a house next spring to live in but he told me to stay on out here for the time being. It's warm and dry and does for me.

SARAH   Have you been here long?

FENTRY   No'm. I was raised thirty miles from here on a cotton farm I worked with my Daddy. My Mama is dead; my Daddy is on the farm all alone now. *(pause)* You from around here?

SARAH   Sort of. Off and on, that is. My husband never cared much for this county and he was always trying to find work away from here. But, we always had to come back.

FENTRY   You on your way home now?

SARAH   No. No, sir.

FENTRY   Were you going to the store at Frenchman's Bend? If you was, you sit right here and I'll go and get whatever it was you wanted.

SARAH   Oh, no, no, sir. I wasn't going to no store.

FENTRY   Were you going into Jefferson?

SARAH   No. No, sir. I wasn't going no place. I was just going.

FENTRY   *(Nods.)* Is your husband dead?

SARAH   No, sir. He just disappeared about three months ago when he first heard about the baby coming.

FENTRY   Don't you have any people?

SARAH   I got a Papa, three brothers.

FENTRY   Can't you go home to them?

SARAH   No, sir. They asked me to leave and never come back after I married my husband. I don't ever intend to go back again. My Papa has his pride; I got mine, too. *(pause)* I don't care a whole lot for the wintertime, do you?

FENTRY   No, ma'm.

SARAH   I always get sick every wintertime it seems to me. A woman came over to where I was staying and said you look poorly. You ought to get a doctor. I said there ain't nothing wrong with me that sunshine couldn't fix, I said.

FENTRY   Do you want me to put some more wood on the fire?

SARAH   No, it's just fine. *(She rubs her hands together.)* I love sunshine. When I started out this morning, I said I'm going, if my strength holds out, till I come to where it's warm and the sun is shining. *(pause)* Well, my strength didn't hold out very long.

The sound of wind whistles around the boiler room.

SARAH   Listen to that wind. I love to hear it when I'm inside and warm. Oh, but that wind was cold though, walking right into it the way I had to.

SARAH *walks over to a corner of the room and stands with her back to* FENTRY.

SARAH   Lord, what's the matter with me? Would you look at me tremble? Just the thought of that wind and I get to shaking and trembling.

FENTRY *goes to her.*

FENTRY   Why don't you rest over here on the bed? Now you can't rest good like that.

SARAH   No, no. I can't stay.

She turns to go out the door, then becomes weak and pauses.

FENTRY   Just for a minute.

SARAH   Well, all right then. Just for a minute.

SARAH *turns slowly. She goes to the bed and sits down.*

SARAH   This does feel good, Mr. . . .

FENTRY   Fentry. Jackson Fentry. And you're Mrs. . . .

SARAH   Eubanks. Sarah Eubanks. I was a Thorpe, but I married a Eubanks. *(She lies down.)* If I have a girl, I'm going to name her Vesta, after my Mama. If I have a boy, I wanted him named *(pause)* . . . Well, I don't know now. I was going to name him after my husband, but I don't know now.

Again the sound of wind whips around the boiler room shed.

SARAH   Listen to that wind whipping around outside again. It sounds right friendly, don't it, when you're inside and warm this way listening to it. When I was a little girl of ten my Mama died, and they say I got everything mixed up that year because I grieved so, and I would wake all winter long, and when the wind would blow around my house, I would think it was my Mama calling and I would answer and call back to her and ask her where she was hiding. I never grieved no more after that. When I got over that, I vowed nothing would break my heart ever again and it didn't for the longest kind of time.

She drifts to sleep. Close up of FENTRY.

DISSOLVE TO

EXTERIOR   COUNTRY ROAD

FENTRY *rides down the road on the mule. He passes in front of a house where several large dogs are barking. Three young men with rifles under their arms pass by.* FENTRY *rides on to a country store. Here he gets off the mule and hitches the reins to a post.*

CUT TO

INTERIOR   COUNTRY STORE

A woman is sitting in the corner warming her hands by a pot-bellied stove. Camera pans across a row of dry goods. A woman storekeeper behind the counter greets FENTRY *as he enters.*

STOREKEEPER   Hello, Fentry.

FENTRY   Hello.

STOREKEEPER   I thought you was going to your farm for Christmas.

FENTRY   I changed my mind.

STOREKEEPER   Well, where are you going?

FENTRY   No place.

FENTRY *looks down at the candy counter.*

FENTRY   How much is that hard candy?

STOREKEEPER   Well, it depends on how much you want to buy.

FENTRY   How much would four cents get me?

The woman dips into the candy and holds up four cents' worth.

STOREKEEPER   I'd say this would do it.

FENTRY   Give me four cents' worth.

The woman puts the candy in a sack and hands it to FENTRY.

STOREKEEPER   Thank you. Merry Christmas.

FENTRY *turns to leave.*

DISSOLVE TO

EXTERIOR   WOODS   NIGHT

We see a shot of the evening sky and hear the hooting of an owl.

CUT TO

INTERIOR   BOILER ROOM

SARAH *is asleep on Fentry's cot.* FENTRY *puts more wood on the fire.* SARAH *wakes up.*

SARAH   Fentry?

FENTRY *turns toward her.*

FENTRY   Yes, ma'm.

SARAH   How long have I been asleep?

FENTRY   About ten hours.

SARAH   Ten hours?

FENTRY   Yes'm.

SARAH   Why didn't you wake me?

FENTRY   I figured the sleep would be good for you.

SARAH   My heavens. Is it still cold out yonder?

FENTRY   Yes, it is. *(He lights a kerosene lantern.)* Why don't you stay on here the rest of the night?

SARAH   Well . . .

FENTRY   I can make a pallet on the floor here, by the fire.

SARAH   Well, thank you. I wouldn't want to put you out any.

FENTRY   You won't be putting me out.

FENTRY *hands* SARAH *the sack of hard candy.*

FENTRY   I went to the store and bought you this. I thought you might like it.

SARAH   I sure do thank you.

She opens the sack.

SARAH   It's hard candy. Well, I declare.

FENTRY *speaks with his back to her.*

FENTRY   Merry Christmas.

SARAH   Thank you. And a Merry Christmas to you, too.

FENTRY   If I fixed you something to eat now, would you eat it?

SARAH   No, I'm still not hungry. I'll just have a taste of my Christmas—(*She begins to cry.*)

FENTRY   What are you crying for, lady?

SARAH   I don't know. I'm just tired and nervous I guess. I've been crying a lot lately. It don't mean nothing, I quit as soon as I start. (*She wipes her eyes.*) You see, I never used to cry before. When I was a girl everyone used to accuse me of being hard hearted because nothing could get me to cry. When my Papa told me I had to leave home after I married my husband, I didn't shed a tear. I said if that's how it has to be that is how it has to be. But lately that's all changed. Somebody'd come up to me and say good morning or good evening and I'll cry. They ask me what time it is and I'll cry. Did you ever hear of anything like that? I didn't use to talk this way either. I used to go a whole day without saying a word. And now I can't stand it silent or quiet.

She opens the candy and takes a piece.

SARAH   Oh, this is so good.

She points the sack at FENTRY.

SARAH   Will you have some?

FENTRY   No, thank you.

FENTRY *looks out the window.*

SARAH   Is it going to be a clear night?

FENTRY   Yes'm.

SARAH   Stars?

FENTRY   Yes'm (*pause*) Why don't you stay on out here until after your baby is born? I have enough to eat for us both. It's warm and dry here.

SARAH   Well, Mr. Fentry . . . I don't think . . .

FENTRY   You don't have to answer me now. You just think it over.

SARAH   Yes, sir.

Close-up of SARAH.

DISSOLVE TO

EXTERIOR   SAWMILL   MORNING

We see woods and the sawmill in the background and we hear the sound of wood being chopped.

INTERIOR   BOILER ROOM

SARAH *opens her eyes. We see a shot of the window.* SARAH *leans up in bed.*

SARAH   Mr. Fentry?

She gets up and puts on her shoes. She picks up a bundle of personal items and goes over to a mirror and looks at herself. She looks out the window at FENTRY *chopping wood. Instrumental music starts up as* SARAH *holds her hand up to the window where the sunlight is streaming in. She takes off her blouse and washes herself.*

EXTERIOR   WOODS

A brief shot of FENTRY *chopping wood.*

INTERIOR   BOILER ROOM

SARAH *reacts to a sudden wave of pain. She sits down by the stove.* FENTRY *walks in with an armload of wood. She quickly turns and slips on her blouse. Music fades.*

SARAH   Good morning.

FENTRY   Morning. How are you feeling?

SARAH   Better, thank you. It's still Christmas ain't it?

FENTRY   Yes, ma'm.

SARAH   I hoped I hadn't slept clear through Christmas. It's a pretty day for Christmas. *(She stands up.)* I'm feeling stronger.

SARAH *walks over to the table. She rests against it, then walks to the stove.*

SARAH   Now let me finish doing that.

FENTRY   No, ma'm. You rest on today. You can do it tomorrow.

FENTRY *brings the food for their plates. He pours the coffee. They sit down and bow their heads for a moment of silent prayer.* SARAH *and* FENTRY *glance at each other as they begin to eat.* FENTRY *sees that* SARAH *is just picking at what's there.*

FENTRY   Ain't you hungry?

SARAH   No, not too hungry.

FENTRY   Bet you will be though, once you're rested.

SARAH *nods.*

DISSOLVE

We hear the sound of an evening thunderstorm.

DISSOLVE TO

INTERIOR   BOILER ROOM   NIGHT

Close up of raindrops. SARAH *looks out the window at the rain. She is wearing a nightgown. She warms herself by the stove and slowly strokes her stomach.* FENTRY *enters with an armload of wood.* FENTRY *unloads the wood and warms his feet. We hear a cloudburst.*

SARAH   It's rained every blessed day for a month.

FENTRY *sits on the table listening.*

SARAH   When I was a girl, I had my own tub to catch rain water. I liked to wash my hair in the rainwater; it made it soft. (SARAH *grinds coffee.*) Can you swin?

FENTRY   No'm.

SARAH   I can't either. It's a good thing we don't live on the Delta. We'd just have to get up on top of this house and float away in case it flooded. Well, I don't think I'd care to travel by water. I think I always want to be where I can feel the ground under my feet. Jesus walked on water, they say. Do you believe that? I knew a preacher once; he swore it was true and he said he was gonna do it, too. A whole crowd of folks went down to watch him, but he sank to the bottom. They say God is gonna destroy the world next time by fire. So I guess we don't have to worry about this rain being the end of the world. I used to not sleep some nights worrying about what I'd do when the world come to an end, what it would be like. I don't worry about that no more.

She goes to the window and looks out.

DISSOLVE TO SPRING FLOWERS.

EXTERIOR YARD DAY

SARAH *is seated in a chair. She has a blanket around her. She watches* FENTRY *as he boils clothes in a large iron pot.* FENTRY *comes over to her.*

FENTRY   You're not getting cold, are you?

SARAH   Aw no, it's much warmer today. It'll be spring before we know it. (*She hums "Buy me a china doll."*) I'll have the baby by then. I wonder where I'll be after it's spring. (*pause*) I wonder if it's going to be a boy or a girl? (*She hums again.*)

FENTRY *doesn't look up, but continues to stir the clothes in the pot.*

FENTRY   Marry me, Sarah.

SARAH *stands up and walks away. She looks back at* FENTRY.

SARAH   Well, I can't marry you, Mr. Fentry. I've got a husband. It's against the law to marry until . . . (*pause*) You gonna stay on here?

FENTRY *hangs clothes on the line.*

FENTRY   I hope to. Mr. Russell says he's gonna build me a

Fentry reveals his love for Sarah in this poignant scene outside the cabin.

house. When you're strong, I'll show you the place I got picked out.

SARAH   Is it far from here?

FENTRY   No'm.

SARAH   I'd like to go and see it.

DISSOLVE TO

EXTERIOR   WOODS

FENTRY *walks through the woods;* SARAH *follows. They walk through the woods until they come to a clearing.* FENTRY *stops.* SARAH *comes up beside him. A slight wind blows through the trees and* SARAH *pulls her shawl around her.*

SARAH   Oh, what a pretty place for a house. Did you ever build a house before?

FENTRY   No'm.

SARAH   How are you gonna build this one?

FENTRY   Mr. Russell and his boy will help me.

SARAH   There was a house in Jefferson we used to pass going into town every Saturday.

They sit down on the grass.

SARAH   I used to like to think I'd live in a house like that someday.

FENTRY   What kind of a house was it?

SARAH   Oh, it was a fine house. It was painted white. It had a gallery all along the front and the side. There were oak trees in the yard; it always looked so peaceful when we passed by. I never saw nobody going in or out. I asked my Papa what kind of people lived there. No better'n you, he said and he hit me. I never knew why he hit me. *(She looks away.)* It would be nice when you have your house if you'd have some of them trees in your yard. My Papa didn't have any trees in our yard. There was no trees, no flowers, no grass, there was nothing. *(She laughs.)* I love grass and flowers and trees. I love honey-suckle and forget-me-nots. And roses. All kinds of roses.

FENTRY   Maybe one day we can ride into Jefferson and see that house.

SARAH   Maybe.

SARAH *unfastens a safety pin and repins it to cover the tear in* FENTRY's *shirt. She gently touches his shoulder. They look into each other's eyes. She looks around. The sun goes behind a cloud casting a shadow over the earth.* SARAH *pulls her shawl around her.*

Robert Duvall portrayed Jackson Fentry.

SARAH   I hate to see the sun go behind the clouds.

She looks up at the sky, then at FENTRY. *He turns away.*

SARAH   I better be getting back.

She starts down the path. FENTRY *follows.*

FADE IN

INTERIOR   BOILER ROOM

Theme music picks up. SARAH *sits by the window wait-ing. It is very quiet. After a moment she gets up and puts her shawl on and exits.*

Olga Bellin played Sarah Eubanks.

EXTERIOR YARD LATE AFTERNOON

SARAH *looks down the road. It is still and quiet in the woods. She goes back into the boiler room.*

INTERIOR BOILER ROOM

SARAH *enters. She bends her head down and looks out the window. She goes back outside.*

EXTERIOR YARD

SARAH *comes out of the boiler room. She nervously glances off towards the road that leads away from the sawmill.* FENTRY *appears. He is riding a mule. Music fades out.* SARAH *smiles at* FENTRY *and gently pats the mule's head as* FENTRY *dismounts and unloads a sack of groceries.*

FENTRY   I was on the way to the store and Mr. Chet Russell asked me to do a favor for him while I was that way. Fellow I had to see wasn't home and I had to wait for him. That's how come I took so long.

SARAH *shivers from the cold.*

FENTRY   You'd better get on back in the house. It's cold out today.

SARAH *turns toward the boiler room.* FENTRY *leads the mule toward the shed.*

INTERIOR   BOILER ROOM

SARAH *is sitting by the stove.* FENTRY *enters.*

FENTRY   Are you warm enough in here?

SARAH   Yes, sir.

FENTRY *puts the groceries away.*

SARAH   I don't think this winter is ever going to end, do you?

FENTRY   Yes, ma'am, it will end one day. I hope I didn't cause you to worry.

SARAH   Oh, I'll find a way to worry, I guess. Nothing you can do about that. I didn't know why you were gone so long. How far is that store, I said. I thought he is just tired of me being out here. Maybe I'm too much trouble. I'm down one day and I'm up the next. But that's not like Mr. Fentry, I said, *(pause)* Then I thought, well, what if my time comes and he ain't here yet. I began to wonder what I'd do if I had to have the baby out here all by myself. You'd left me plenty of stove wood, I saw that right away. I didn't really think you'd gone off, it's just that it got so quiet here and I . . .

FENTRY *goes to her.*

FENTRY   Marry me, Sarah.

SARAH   I can't marry you. I've told you that. I got a husband somewhere.

FENTRY   He's deserted you.

SARAH   I can't help that. We're married in the sight of the law.

ISHAM   Hey, Fentry!

> ISHAM RUSSELL *enters the boiler room. He is carrying a shotgun over his shoulder. He sees* SARAH *and stops abruptly.*

ISHAM   I'm sorry, Fentry. I didn't know you had company.

EXTERIOR   YARD

> ISHAM *exits the boiler room followed by* FENTRY.

ISHAM   Who is that?

FENTRY   She's my wife.

ISHAM   Since when? You didn't have no wife when I was out here Christmas Eve. You didn't . . .

FENTRY   She's my wife. You want us to leave?

ISHAM   What do I want you to leave for? I don't care what you do out here. You can have twenty wives out here for all I care. I didn't come out here to spy on you. I just came to get you to go hunting.

FENTRY   Some other time.

ISHAM   All right. *(He walks away, then turns back.)* Pa wanted me to ask you to pick out the site of where you want your house. You and me can get started on it this spring.

FENTRY   I know where I want it to be.

ISHAM   Why don't you show me while I'm out here and if we have a warm day anytime soon, I can get Papa to come out and look it over.

FENTRY   All right.

FENTRY *and* ISHAM *start out walking toward the woods.*

INTERIOR   BOILER ROOM

SARAH *watches them leave, then turns back to the cabinets.*

EXTERIOR   WOODS

ISHAM *and* FENTRY *are walking through the woods.*

INTERIOR   BOILER ROOM

SARAH *experiences a quick seizure of pain. She sits down by the stove. She sings a snatch of a song to herself, "Mama buy me a china doll, Mama buy me a china doll, Mama buy me a china doll. Do Mama do." She has another spasm of pain. She grasps the chair and the pain subsides. She resumes singing, "What will it take to buy, What will it take to buy, . . ."*

CUT TO

EXTERIOR   WOODS

FENTRY *and* ISHAM *walk through the woods to the clearing where the house is to be.* FENTRY *marks off the perimeter of the house.* SARAH *hums voice-over "do mama do . . ." Theme music picks up softly and fades out.*

CUT TO

INTERIOR   BOILER ROOM

SARAH *gets out of the chair and goes to the door. She doesn't see* FENTRY *and starts back inside, towards the bed. On the way, she has a quick seizure of pain. She winces, pauses and then goes back to the door.*

SARAH   Fentry! Fentry!

EXTERIOR   WOODS

FENTRY *comes running through the woods, followed by* ISHAM.

INTERIOR   BOILER ROOM

FENTRY *enters the boiler room.* SARAH *is leaning against the table.*

SARAH   It's time. You'd better get Mrs. Hulie.

FENTRY   I will.

> FENTRY *hurries out the door.*

EXTERIOR   YARD

> ISHAM *is standing by.* FENTRY *comes out of the boiler room.*

FENTRY   Will you do a favor for me?

ISHAM   Sure.

FENTRY   Will you ride over to Mrs. Hulie's, the midwife, and tell her to come out here right away?

ISHAM   I'll be glad to.

> ISHAM *hurries off.* FENTRY *goes back into the boiler room.*

INTERIOR   BOILER ROOM

> SARAH *is lying on the bed.* FENTRY *goes to her.*

FENTRY   I got Isham to go for me.

SARAH   Who's he?

FENTRY   The fellow that came up just now. His pa owns the sawmill.

SARAH   Was he surprised to see me here?

FENTRY   I reckon.

SARAH   Did he ask who I was?

FENTRY   Yes'm.

SARAH   What did you tell him?

FENTRY   I said you was my wife.

> SARAH *shivers from the cold.*

FENTRY   Are you cold again?

SARAH   Yes, all of a sudden. Is there some wood in the fire?

FENTRY   Yes, there is. You want me to put some more in?

SARAH   If you don't mind.

FENTRY *puts more wood in the stove.*

FENTRY   It's red hot now. It'll have this room like an oven before too long.

He goes back to SARAH.

SARAH   Did you show him where you wanted your house?

FENTRY   Yes.

SARAH   Did he think it was a nice place?

FENTRY   Yes.

SARAH *has a sudden spasm of pain. She grabs* FENTRY'S *hand and sits beside him.*

SARAH   I'm afraid.

FENTRY   What of?

SARAH   I'm afraid I'm gonna die.

FENTRY   From childbirth? You won't die from that. You'll get up from here feeling just fine. Now, lot of women done that . . .

SARAH   No, I'm not afraid of childbirth . . .

FENTRY   Of what then?

SARAH   I don't know. I'm tired and I'm wore out, and my spirits are low . . .

FENTRY   You'll feel better afterwards, you'll see. Carrying the baby has wore you out.

SARAH *has another seizure of pain.*

SARAH   Fentry. Fentry. (*He holds her.*) I ain't had much in this life, and that's the truth. Work and hunger and pain. I'm afraid. I'm afraid I'm going to die. I don't want to die.

FENTRY   Now, you're not going to die. You hear me, you are not going to die. I won't let you. Now, I promise you. (*He holds her up.*) Are you warmer now?

SARAH   Yes, thank you.

FENTRY   Now you try and get some sleep until Mrs. Hulie gets here.

FENTRY *leads her over to the bed and she lies down.*

SARAH   All right. Don't leave me.

FENTRY   I won't. I ain't going to never leave you, unless you ask me to. Never. Never. Never.

SARAH *closes her eyes.* FENTRY *watches.*

EXTERIOR   MIDWIFE'S HOUSE   NIGHT

ISHAM *drives up in a horse-drawn buggy. We hear a dog barking.*

ISHAM   Whoa! Whoa!

ISHAM *gets out of the buggy and runs to the door.*

ISHAM   Mrs. Hulie! Mrs. Hulie! (*He knocks at the door.*) Mrs. Hulie!

MRS. HULIE *comes to the door with a lantern in her hand.*

ISHAM   Mrs. Hulie, there's a woman over at the sawmill about to have a baby. Can you come with me?

MRS. HULIE   I'll be right there.

MRS. HULIE *shuts the door and in a moment exits the house.* ISHAM *helps* MRS. HULIE *into the buggy.*

DISSOLVE TO

EXTERIOR   SAWMILL

FENTRY *comes out of the boiler room. He walks up the road a short way when he hears the buggy approaching, then he hurries back into the boiler room.*

INTERIOR   BOILER ROOM

FENTRY *enters.* SARAH *is on the bed.*

FENTRY   I hear Isham's buggy.

EXTERIOR   YARD

Buggy drives up.

ISHAM   Whoa! Whoa!

INTERIOR   BOILER ROOM

SARAH turns toward FENTRY.

SARAH   Tell 'em to hurry.

FENTRY   I will.

FENTRY *exits.* SARAH *sits up on the bed; she is breathing heavily.* FENTRY *and* MRS. HULIE *enter.* FENTRY *lights some candles.* MRS. HULIE *goes to* SARAH.

FENTRY   Sarah, Mrs. Hulie is here.

SARAH *opens her eyes.*

MRS. HULIE   Howdy, Mrs.

MRS. HULIE *inspects the water and looks around the room. She opens her satchel.* FENTRY *goes outside.*

EXTERIOR   YARD

ISHAM *is still there with the buggy.* FENTRY *comes out of the boiler room.*

INTERIOR   BOILER ROOM

MRS. HULIE *begins helping* SARAH. SARAH *gasps with pain.*

EXTERIOR   YARD

ISHAM *turns to* FENTRY.

ISHAM   How is she?

FENTRY   She's gonna be all right.

INTERIOR   BOILER ROOM

SARAH *cries with pain as* MRS. HULIE *pulls back the bed-sheets.*

EXTERIOR   YARD

ISHAM *starts to go, then turns back to* FENTRY *who has gone into a lumber shed.*

ISHAM   Fentry. Fentry. You need me for anything else now?

FENTRY   No, thank you.

ISHAM   Well, I'll be going on then.

INTERIOR   BOILER ROOM

MRS. HULIE *rips apart some sheets.* SARAH *moans.* MRS. HULIE *boils the sheets.*

INTERIOR   LUMBER SHED

FENTRY *is sanding a box he has made. We hear* SARAH *screaming for* MRS. HULIE.

INTERIOR   BOILER ROOM

MRS. HULIE *is at the stove getting wet cloths.* SARAH *screams.*

SARAH   Mrs. Hulie! Mrs. Hulie!

MRS. HULIE *goes to* SARAH *and holds her arms.* SARAH *begins to thrash about.* MRS. HULIE *forces a cloth in* SARAH'S *mouth.*

INTERIOR   LUMBER SHED

FENTRY *sands the crib and blows the sawdust off.*

INTERIOR   BOILER ROOM

MRS. HULIE *lifts* SARAH'S *legs, then grips her hands and holds her back.* SARAH *screams. We see a series of close-up shots of* SARAH *screaming.* SARAH'S *head drops back and she stops screaming.*

FADE TO BLACK

FADE IN

EXTERIOR   YARD   MORNING

FENTRY *comes out of the lumber shed with the baby crib.*

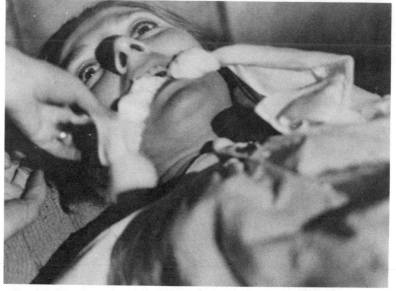

Reva Schlesinger, film editor, points to the post-production assembling of this scene as one of her most challenging tasks as film editor for "Tomorrow."

MRS. HULIE *is kneeling down by a fire outside the boiler room.*

MRS. HULIE   The baby's come. It's a fine boy.

FENTRY   Thank you.

He points to the crib.

FENTRY   I made this for him to sleep in.

FENTRY *starts toward the boiler room.*

MRS. HULIE   Fentry . . .

FENTRY *pauses.* MRS. HULIE *walks over to him.*

MRS. HULIE   Fentry . . .

FENTRY   Yes'm.

MRS. HULIE   I'm worried about the mama. She ain't doing too well. I ain't going to lie to you. She ain't doing good at all.

FENTRY   Yes, ma'm.

MRS. HULIE   She says she's afraid she's going to die and she will never get up off that bed in there. And I hate to tell you this, but I don't think she will either.

FENTRY   What is it? Was it having the baby?

MRS. HULIE   No. She was sick long before she had the baby. She's just played out it seems to me.

FENTRY   Yes, ma'm. Well, I'll take care of her. I'll make her rest and I'll nurse her.

FENTRY *goes into the boiler room.*

INTERIOR   BOILER ROOM

FENTRY *goes to* SARAH's *bedside. He looks down at her. She has the baby beside her.*

SARAH   Ain't it small?

FENTRY   Yes, it is.

FENTRY *takes hold of the baby's hand.*

FENTRY   Hello, son. Welcome.

FENTRY *turns to* SARAH.

FENTRY   Can I get you something to eat?

SARAH   No.

FENTRY   You got to eat. You got to keep your strength up.

SARAH   I'm not hungry.

FENTRY   Can I hold the baby?

SARAH   Sure.

FENTRY *takes the baby in his arms and holds it against his body. He stands up and walks with the baby around the room.*

SARAH   Fentry . . .

FENTRY   Yes'm.

SARAH   If anything happens to me, will you promise to take care of the baby?

FENTRY   Ain't nothing going to happen to you.

SARAH   If it does.

FENTRY   Then you can rest easy. I'll always take care of him.

SARAH   The same as if it was yours?

FENTRY   The same as if it was mine.

SARAH   Thank you. Fentry . . .

FENTRY   Yes?

SARAH   If you still want to marry me, I'm willing now. My husband might be dead for all I know and even if he's not, he's gone so far away I'll never find him again. (*pause*) And I thought why can't Fentry and I get married right now, if he still wants to marry me.

FENTRY   I want to marry you.

SARAH   Can you get anybody to marry us right away?

FENTRY   Yes'm. Preacher Whitehead. He lives about seven miles from here.

SARAH   Would you go get him now?

FENTRY   I will.

FENTRY *gives the baby back to* SARAH.

SARAH   How far does he live?

FENTRY   About seven miles.

SARAH   Thank you. Will you hurry?

FENTRY *leaves immediately.* SARAH *looks down at the baby beside her.*

EXTERIOR   YARD

MRS. HULIE *watches* FENTRY *go by; then she enters the boiler room.*

INTERIOR BOILER ROOM

MRS. HULIE *goes over to* SARAH'S *bed.*

MRS. HULIE You know, I've placed you. Weren't you a Thorpe? Didn't you live with your papa and three brothers on a farm back yonder? Don't you think they should be sent for at a time like this?

SARAH I don't want them to know anything about me.

MRS. HULIE I split some of these flour sacks in two for you. When Mr. Fentry comes back, I'll show him how they can be used for diapers.

SARAH Thank you.

MRS. HULIE *sits down beside the bed.*

MRS. HULIE Have you picked a name for your baby?

SARAH No, I thought I'd let my husband name him.

MRS. HULIE Your husband?

SARAH Mr. Fentry. We're going to be married. He's gone now to get the preacher.

MRS. HULIE That's nice.

MRS. HULIE *reaches for the baby.*

MRS. HULIE Here, let me take the baby. You try and get some sleep now.

SARAH Thank you.

MRS. HULIE *puts the baby in the crib* FENTRY *has made. She hums. Dissolve to* SARAH *sleeping.* MRS. HULIE *has fallen asleep in her chair. Dissolve to* FENTRY *and* PREACHER WHITEHEAD *coming into the room.* FENTRY *lights a lantern and the preacher goes to the fire to warm himself.* FENTRY *goes over to* SARAH'S *bed.*

FENTRY Sarah, I have the preacher here.

SARAH All right.

MRS. HULIE *has awakened. She sees* FENTRY *and the* PREACHER *and gets up.*

MRS. HULIE   Howdy, Preacher.

PREACHER   Hello, Mrs. Hulie *(To Sarah)* Hello, Mrs.

SARAH   Hello, Preacher.

MRS. HULIE   Preacher. *(She whispers something in his ear.)*

> *The* PREACHER *gets out his Bible and stands at the foot of the bed.* MRS. HULIE *stands across from him.* FENTRY *stands beside* SARAH *at the head of the bed.*

PREACHER   Dearly Beloved, we are gathered together here in the sight of God. Jackson Fentry, do you take this woman to be your lawful wedded wife?

FENTRY   Yes, sir.

PREACHER   Mrs.?

SARAH   Sarah Eubanks.

PREACHER   Sarah Eubanks, do you take this man to be your lawful wedded husband?

SARAH   I do.

PREACHER   Then I pronounce you man and wife.

> SARAH *closes her eyes.* MRS. HULIE *leads the* PREACHER *to a corner of the room where they look at the baby.*

SARAH   How is the fire, Fentry?

FENTRY   Are you cold?

SARAH   I'm so cold.

> FENTRY *goes over to the stove and feels it.*

FENTRY   I don't dare put no more wood on it. It's red hot now.

> FENTRY *goes back to the bed and puts a blanket over her. He sits down at her side.*

SARAH   While you were gone, I had a terrible dream that I was freezing to death. In my dream I kept saying, I'm drowning in the cold, I'm drowning in the snow and I was calling to you to save me.

FENTRY   And I didn't save you?

SARAH   I don't know. I woke up when I was calling you and there you were standing right by me.

FENTRY   When I brought the preacher here I passed by the place where our house is going to be. I don't reckon I can build as fine a one as you seen in Jefferson but ours is going to have three rooms and a little porch for us to sit on. It'll have some pretty trees all around it like you want, a hackberry tree and a chinaberry. And there will be some flowers in the yard if you want them.

SARAH   Will you get me the baby?

FENTRY   Yes, ma'm. Are you all right?

SARAH   Yes. Just get my baby, please.

FENTRY *goes over to the crib and gets the baby. He comes back to* SARAH *and is about to give the baby to her when he looks down at her face. Her eyes are closed.*

FENTRY   Sarah, I have the baby here for you. Sarah . . . Mrs. Hulie! Preacher Whitehead!

MRS. HULIE *and the* PREACHER *come to the bedside.* MRS. HULIE *feels* SARAH'S *heart.*

MRS. HULIE   She's dead.

FENTRY   No, she's not going to die. She is going to be all right, because I'm going to save her.

MRS. HULIE   You can't save her. She's dead.

FENTRY *doesn't protest any longer. He stands looking at* SARAH. MRS. HULIE *takes the baby from him. The* PREACHER *puts his hand on* FENTRY'S *shoulder for a moment.* MRS. HULIE *puts the baby back in the crib and leads the* PREACHER *out the door.* FENTRY *sits next to* SARAH.

FENTRY   I don't know why we met when we did or why I found you when you was all wore out, and I couldn't save you no matter how bad I wanted to. I don't know why you wanted me to raise this baby instead of your people. I don't know what they done to you to make you turn so on them. But I don't care. I promised you I'd raise him and I will. Like he was my own.

FENTRY *straightens the blankets over* SARAH. *He picks up her shawl and holds on to it. He goes over to the crib and looks down at the baby.*

FENTRY   Your Mama is dead, son. But I'm gonna take care of you and see to you. I'll be your Mama and your Papa. You'll never want or do without while I have a breath of life in my bones.

FENTRY *exits.*

EXTERIOR   YARD   DAYLIGHT

The PREACHER *and* MRS. HULIE *are standing together.* FENTRY *closes the outside window and walks over to the* PREACHER *and* MRS. HULIE.

FENTRY   I'm going to take the baby and go back to my farm today.

MRS. HULIE   Have you ever taken care of a baby before?

FENTRY   No'm.

MRS. HULIE   You know, you're gonna have to find a way to feed it. A cow's expensive to keep in the winter even if you had the money to buy one. I think you ought to get a goat to feed your baby.

FENTRY   Yes, ma'm.

MRS. HULIE   I got one I'll sell you cheap.

FENTRY   I sure do thank you.

MRS. HULIE   Do you know anything about goats?

FENTRY   No, ma'm.

MRS. HULIE   Well, a goat ain't like a cow. You got to milk it every two hours.

FENTRY   Yes'm.

MRS. HULIE   And that is nights too.

FENTRY   Yes'm.

PREACHER   When do you want the funeral?

FENTRY   Right away.

DISSOLVE TO

EXTERIOR   WOODS

FENTRY *and* PREACHER WHITEHEAD *are carrying* SARAH'S *body in a wooden coffin.* MRS. HULIE *follows after them. She holds the baby wrapped in a blanket.*

DISSOLVE TO

EXTERIOR   GRAVE

SARAH'S *coffin has been placed in the grave. It is the spot where* FENTRY *wanted his house.* MRS. HULIE, PREACHER WHITEHEAD *and* FENTRY *stand beside the open grave. The* PREACHER *reads from his Bible.*

PREACHER   I am the resurrection and the life; he that believeth in me, though he were dead, yet shall he live; and whosoever liveth and believeth in me shall never die. Believest thou this? Amen.

DISSOLVE TO

EXTERIOR   SAWMILL

FENTRY *gets in the buggy next to* ISHAM. *A goat is hitched to the back of the buggy.* FENTRY *is holding the baby in its wooden cradle. As they start out, theme music picks up.*

DISSOLVE TO

EXTERIOR   ROAD

The buggy comes down the road and stops. FENTRY *gets out and milks the goat. Dissolve to a moving shot of the buggy going down the road.* FENTRY *sits next to* ISHAM *and feeds the baby from a bottle.*

*Isham Russell, played by Richard McConnell, takes Fentry and the
infant boy back to the Fentry farm after the death of Sarah.*

DISSOLVE TO

EXTERIOR   FENTRY FARM

The buggy approaches the FENTRY *farm.* PAPA FENTRY
comes out of a frame house as FENTRY *and* ISHAM *get out
of the buggy.* FENTRY *is holding the baby. He walks toward his father. Music fades out.*

FENTRY   Hello, Papa.

PAPA   Hello, Fentry.

FENTRY   I'm home.

PAPA   I see you are.

FENTRY   I'm home for good.

PAPA   Is that so?

FENTRY   Yes, sir. This is Isham Russell. His daddy owns the sawmill I worked in.

ISHAM   Howdy, Mr. Fentry.

PAPA   Howdy.

ISHAM *and* PAPA FENTRY *shake hands.*

PAPA   I was looking for you Christmas Day, Fentry.

FENTRY   Yes, sir, I know. I couldn't get here Christmas Day.

PAPA FENTRY *looks down at the baby.*

PAPA   Who does that belong to?

FENTRY   Me. It's my baby, Papa. I got married.

PAPA   Where's your wife?

FENTRY   She died.

PAPA FENTRY *looks down at the baby.*

PAPA   What'd you name it?

FENTRY   Well, I thought I would name it after the two generals you served under. Jackson and Longstreet. If it's all right with you.

PAPA   It's fine with me.

PAPA FENTRY *takes the baby in his arms.*

PAPA   Come over here to me, Jackson and Longstreet Fentry.

FENTRY *unties the goat from the back of the buggy. He holds the cradle under his arm.*

ISHAM   You don't need me for nothing else, so I guess I'll be getting on back home.

FENTRY   I sure thank you.

ISHAM   That's all right. Good luck.

They shake hands.

FENTRY   Good luck to you.

ISHAM *gets in the buggy and drives off.*

FADE TO BLACK

FADE IN

EXTERIOR   FENTRY FARM

A montage of shots showing FENTRY's *life with the young boy begins. Theme music picks up in a lively tempo. We see the baby in a papoose hanging on the side of the house.* LAWYER DOUGLAS *returns as voice-over narrator.*

LAWYER (VO)   And Fentry raised that boy.

FENTRY *picks up the papoose. Dissolve to* FENTRY *working in the cotton fields with the papoose on his back.*

LAWYER (VO)   He did everything for Jackson and Longstreet himself.

Dissolve to FENTRY *hanging up a pot. The boy is in the papoose on* FENTRY's *back. Dissolve to the cotton fields.* FENTRY *carries the boy—now about four years old—on his shoulders.*

LAWYER (VO)   Sometimes, his neighbors said, he seemed to begrudge the earth itself for what the boy had to eat to stay alive.

Dissolve to boy in the fields picking cotton. FENTRY *is also picking. They empty their sacks into a cotton wagon. They play on the wagon. Boy sits between* FENTRY *and* PAPA FENTRY *as they haul the cotton off. Cut to the interior of the* FENTRY *cabin.* FENTRY *and the boy kneel in prayer. They climb into bed together. Cut to the boy running through the field, chasing* FENTRY. *Cut to a road on rainy day. The boy plays barefooted in a puddle while* FENTRY *looks on. Cut to boy riding a mule led by* FENTRY. *Dissolve to* FENTRY *lifting the boy onto the porch.*

DISSOLVE TO

Fentry's devotion to Sarah's child is revealed in a montage of grow-ing-up scenes with the boy, played by the son of a local farmer.

EXTERIOR CREEK

FENTRY *is in his long underwear. He and the boy wade into a shallow creek.*

FENTRY   Come on. I'm going to learn you how. Come on.

JACKSON AND LONGSTREET   The water's too cold.

FENTRY   It ain't cold. Come on. Come on.

JACKSON AND LONGSTREET   I think it's cold.

FENTRY *splashes. The boy splashes back.*

FENTRY   Don't fall. *(They splash each other.)* Stop. You think I can catch a fish. Huh? What kind you want me to catch?

JACKSON AND LONGSTREET   A catfish. A little one. We can cook him.

FENTRY   Watch me now. This is the way you catch—

FENTRY *falls in the creek. The boy laughs.*

DISSOLVE TO

EXTERIOR   FENTRY FARM

The boy wanders into a plot of graves. FENTRY *is at a distance.*

FENTRY   Jackson and Longstreet, come out of them graves there.

Boy runs across the field to FENTRY.

FENTRY   I told you to stay out of them graves.

JACKSON AND LONGSTREET   What's in a grave?

Boy climbs over the fence to FENTRY.

FENTRY   That's where you bury people.

JACKSON AND LONGSTREET   What people?

FENTRY   My Mama and her Mama.

JACKSON AND LONGSTREET   Where is my Mama?

FENTRY   Someplace else. Bet I can spit further than you can.

They spit at the ground. FENTRY *looks up at the sky. We see a shot of a hawk in the sky.* FENTRY *takes the boy in his arms.*

FENTRY   Look up yonder, boy. Look up there. You know what that is flying around?

JACKSON AND LONGSTREET   Un-un.

FENTRY   That's a chicken hawk. You know what they do?

JACKSON AND LONGSTREET   Un-un.

FENTRY   Catch and kill your chickens if you got any. And someday when you're big enough, I'm going to get you a gun and we'll shoot chicken hawks together.

FENTRY *puts the boy down.*

FENTRY   You run along and play, boy, while your Daddy finishes his work. Stay here in the yard.

FENTRY *takes his mule and starts off toward the fields. From up the road we hear the sound of wagon wheels and horses' hooves.* ISHAM *is on horseback, followed by three men in a wagon. The boy runs out to them, then runs back down toward the field where* FENTRY *has headed. The men stop and get out.* FENTRY *walks up. The boy is behind him.*

ISHAM   Howdy, Fentry.

FENTRY   Howdy.

ISHAM   You remember me?

FENTRY   Yes, I do.

ISHAM   How you been?

FENTRY   Pretty fair. How you been?

ISHAM   All right. That your boy?

FENTRY   Yes, sir.

ISHAM   Hi, boy.

FENTRY   Say hello to Mr. Isham, son.

JACKSON AND LONGSTREET   Hello.

ISHAM *points to the three men behind him.*

ISHAM   These here are your wife's brothers, Bud, Les, and Billy Thorpe.

FENTRY   Howdy. What can I do for you?

LES   We've come for the boy.

FENTRY   What boy?

LES   That boy.

FENTRY   You can't have him. He's my boy.

LES   We're gonna have him.

FENTRY   He's my boy.

LES   He's our sister's boy. His Daddy gave him to us. He's our kin. He belongs to us.

Boy begins to cry. FENTRY *pushes the boy aside.*

FENTRY   Run, boy. Run to the fields to your grandpap.

FENTRY *picks up a long-handled object and starts for the nearest* THORPE. *He leaps over a log and falls.* FENTRY *begins a fierce struggle as all three men try to hold him down.* ISHAM *struggles to release him. The boy picks up a piece of stove wood and runs toward the strange men. He hits one of them.*

FENTRY   Run, boy. Run, boy.

LES   Bud, grab the boy.

BILLY   Don't let that boy get away.

The boy fights and kicks at BUD *to keep him away, but the man grabs his arms and carries the boy to the wagon.* FENTRY *continues his struggle against the other men.*

FENTRY   Jackson and Longstreet. Jackson and Longstreet. Jackson and Longstreet.

ISHAM   Fentry. Fentry, stop it. There ain't nothing you can do for him now. They got the law on their side.

There is no answer. We hear the heavy breathing of the struggling men, then FENTRY *collapses.* ISHAM *and the two* BROTHERS *leave him lying on the ground.*

ISHAM   They can take the boy, Fentry. It's the law. Her husband, he's still alive and he gave the boy to them. I didn't want to bring them here, Fentry. But the sheriff said if I didn't, he'd find you.

FENTRY   I knew it. I been expecting it. I reckon that's why it took me so by surprise. *(pause)* I'm all right now.

FENTRY *moans. He is still on the ground.* LES *stands over him.*

LES   We're sorry for it, but he's our kin. We want him home. Here, here's some money for your trouble.

LES *takes a coin purse out of his pocket and puts it into* FENTRY's *hand.* LES *gets in the wagon beside his brother and they drive off with the boy.* ISHAM *sits on the ground beside* FENTRY *until the* THORPE BROTHERS *have disappeared down the road.*

ISHAM   They're gone.

FENTRY *glances vacantly at the coin purse and tosses it on the ground. He gets up.*

ISHAM   The sheriff, he came with them to the sawmill, Fentry. They had a paper. Look, Fentry, there's two sides to the law. We'll go into town, see Colonel Douglas. My Pa knows him. Look, Fentry, I'll go with you. I'll ask him to take care of it for you.

FENTRY *walks across the yard to the gate that leads to the fields.* ISHAM *follows.*

ISHAM   Fentry . . .

FENTRY *keeps walking and doesn't answer him. As* FENTRY *walks toward the fields the lawyer's voice-over narration picks up again.*

LAWYER DOUGLAS (VO)   My search was almost over when I found they took the boy, left the county with him and raised him as a Thorpe. And it seemed to me, as if I'd never known before that this world isn't run like it ought to be run.

DISSOLVE TO FENTRY HOEING IN THE FIELD.

LAWYER (VO)   Fentry didn't hear any more of the boy. And as far as I could learn . . .

DISSOLVE TO FENTRY PICKING COTTON.

LAWYER (VO)   . . . never mentioned his name again. Fentry's father died and he worked the place alone.

DISSOLVE TO FENTRY BEHIND A PLOW.

LAWYER (VO)   And then one day a young man named Buck Thorpe appeared in Frenchman's Bend.

EXTERIOR   COURTHOUSE

We return to trial scene shown in the beginning of the film. We hear the lawyer addressing the jury.

LAWYER (VO)   When Thorpe tried to run away with H. T. Bookwright's daughter Bookwright warned him that he would protect her.

INTERIOR   COURTROOM

The lawyer is addressing the jury.

LAWYER   And he solved that problem to the best of his abilities and beliefs, asking the help of no man, and then abode by his decision.

We sight FENTRY *among the jurors. His face is without expression.*

DISSOLVE TO:

EXTERIOR   FENTRY FARM

We go back to a few brief scenes of JACKSON AND LONG- STREET FENTRY *as a young boy. He is on the front porch of the* FENTRY *cabin.*

LAWYER (VO)   Buck Thorpe had been in a lot of trouble.

The boy is in the field picking cotton with FENTRY.

LAWYER (VO)   There was talk of his killing a man himself in Memphis. We know he was a fraud. He was a drinker and a cattle thief.

EXTERIOR   H. T. BOOKWRIGHT'S
HOUSE   NIGHT

We return to the scene of the elopement attempt. BUCK THORPE *pulls out a gun and* BOOKWRIGHT *fires a shotgun.* THORPE *collapses.*

DISSOLVE TO

INTERIOR   JURORS' ROOM

We return to the jury deliberation. The members are lounging around the room. The foreman paces the room. We see a closeup of FENTRY'S *solemn face.*

1ST JUROR   Buck Thorpe deserved what he got.

2ND JUROR   I would have shot him if it had been my girl.

3RD JUROR I tell you, I wouldn't have waited as long as Bookwright did.

The FOREMAN *approaches* FENTRY.

FOREMAN He was not only no good, but dangerous.

FENTRY Yes, sir.

FOREMAN Then what do you want? What do you want?

FENTRY I can't help it. I ain't going to vote Bookwright free.

INTERIOR   COURTROOM

The JUDGE *holds up his gavel.*

JUDGE I declare a mistrial.

Spectators rush out of the courtroom and down the steps of the courthouse. FENTRY *is the last one down.*

EXTERIOR   COURTHOUSE

FENTRY *comes out of the courthouse and crosses a road. He unhitches his mule. The* LAWYER *silently watches* FENTRY *leave.*

LAWYER (VO) Of course, Fentry wasn't going to vote Bookwright free, because somewhere in Buck Thorpe, the adult, the man that Bookwright slew, there still remained at least the memory of that little boy, Jackson and Longstreet.

The LAWYER *watches* FENTRY *get on his mule.*

LAWYER (VO) I could never have guessed Fentry's capacity for love. I suppose I'd figured, coming from where he came from, even the comprehension of love had been lost out of him back down the generations where the first Fentry had to take his final choice between the pursuit of love and the pursuit of keeping on breathing.

The LAWYER *looks on.*

LAWYER (VO) The lowly and invincible of the earth, to endure and endure, and then endure . . .

FENTRY *rides past a building in the town.*

Joseph Anthony, the director of the film, "discovered" this court-house in a tiny Mississippi township called Jacinto.

DISSOLVE TO

EXTERIOR ROAD

FENTRY *rides his mule as* LAWYER *completes narration.*

LAWYER (VO)   Tomorrow and tomorrow and tomorrow.

FENTRY *passes by on his mule. Freeze-frame on woods as credits roll.*

Jackson Fentry	ROBERT DUVALL
Sarah Eubanks	OLGA BELLIN
Mrs. Hulie	SUDIE BOND
Isham Russell	RICHARD MCCONNELL
Lawyer Douglas	PETER MASTERSON

Papa Fentry	WILLIAM HAWLEY
Preacher Whitehead	JAMES FRANKS
Jackson and Longstreet	JOHNNY MASK
Storekeeper	EFFIE GREEN
Judge	KEN LINDLEY
Jury Foreman	R. M. WEAVER
Buck Thorpe	DICK DOUGHERTY
H. T. Bookwright	JEFF WILLIAMS
Thorpe Brothers	JACK SMILEY
	BILLY SUMMERFORD
	THOMAS C. COGGIN

The producers gratefully acknowledge the invaluable assistance and cooperation of the city of Tupelo, Lee County, the Community Development Foundation in Tupelo, and the Oakland Community in Itawamba County, Mississippi.

FADE TO BLACK

CONVERSATIONS WITH THE FILM'S CREATORS

THE ESSAYS in this section were adapted from interviews the editors conducted with the principal creators of the film. In a three-way telephone conference interview Horton Foote, Paul Roebling, and Olga Bellin discussed the film with students in David Yellin's graduate seminar in comparative media at Memphis State University. The editors interviewed Joseph Anthony, Gilbert Pearlman, Reva Schlesinger, Robert Duvall, and Horton Foote individually.

THE VISUAL TAKES OVER
Horton Foote

SOMETIME during 1968, Herbert Berghof, a director who runs a theatre school in New York with his wife, Uta Hagen, called me about doing "Tomorrow" as a play in his small Off-Broadway studio theatre on Bank Street. He wanted to use my play basically as it was done on television with the exception of making Thornton Douglas rather than Pruitt our narrator, and starting the play with Douglas's speech to the jury, or part of it, and having him address the audience as if they were the jury. He was casting Robert Duvall in the role of Fentry and Olga Bellin as Sarah. I have great respect for Herbert's directorial talents and I agreed to let him do it.

I was living in New Hampshire then and only came to a run-through in the last week of rehearsals. I was very impressed with the work of the director and the actors. Paul Roebling and Gilbert Pearlman saw the play on opening night, April 15, 1968, and a few weeks later they called to ask me about doing it as a film and if I would care to do the screenplay. They wanted to use Robert Duvall and Olga Bellin in the two lead parts.

In our first discussion, Paul and Gilbert said that the presence of Sarah Eubanks, which was so felt in the first part of the story as I had dramatized it, should somehow be kept in the second part. So I took that as a kind of task for myself knowing that one would have enormous visual and physical freedom with the camera, not given to me in theatre and live television. They wanted to film on location in Mississippi, and they wanted to make it as authentic as possible, and they said they would do everything they could to maintain that authenticity.

I wrote many new scenes for the film. For instance, only in the film were we able to show the birth of the baby. We took Fentry and Sarah outside the cabin as much as possible, dramatizing the moment when he shows her where he hopes to build her house. We added scenes such as the scene in the store where Fentry buys the hard candy for Sarah, the burial after Sarah dies, Fentry's trip home with the baby and goat; and many new scenes between Fentry and the boy.

In film, the visual, sometimes in subtle ways, really takes over. The visual has an emotional impact that you can't get in the theater and you can get it better on film than on live television. In film, which has its own time and space, it was easier to dramatize the passage of the several years between the time when the boy was taken away from Fentry and when he reappears in the story as a young man and is killed. And film allowed us to have Fentry appear both as a much younger man and also as an older man. In live television, he simply had to stay physically the same.

In the film I had a concept about a beginning, a middle and end for it that was aesthetically pleasing and dramatically sound. And we had wonderful performances. But I don't know that any amount of mental calculation beforehand could have accounted for the way it all turned out. The screenplay we went into rehearsal with had a great deal of material in the second half, trying to keep the memory of Sarah alive. But most of it was cut in rehearsals before the filming began.

My memory is that there were a whole series of accidents that led to the final cut of this film. I saw a version before the final one that I would have gone out and slit my throat had it been the one released. The version that I objected to wasn't done for crass reasons or mercenary reasons. They simply wanted to try something, with all good faith, just like I got into this in the beginning with Playhouse 90 because I wanted to try to do the story of Sarah.

I would be a much wealthier man than I am if I could really say how these things come about. But in all media where there is collaboration—as in theater, TV, and film—for good or bad, you have an improvisational thing happening. A film has its own rhythm, its own life. That's why it's important to work with people that you are sympathetic with. Then you can trust each other. Often, then, the results are good. Sometimes, of course, they don't work. I feel that as a writer, I have to accept the fact that the director, the producers, the actors, the editor, cameraman, and others will each have a point of view. And they each can differ in varying ways from yours and each others. What happened in *Tomorrow* was one of those marvelous things that sometimes happens: everybody was on the same wave length.

I think Faulkner's story is separate and equal and powerful in its own right. I think that each of the other versions tried to become an experience on its own. I think the film is the most complete, on its own, as an experience. I believe that of all of my versions of Faulkner's story, the film is the best.

People often ask my advice about dramatizing Faulkner. I think the first essential is to establish the moral and aesthetic climate of those involved in the production—to be sure the desire to do Faulkner is a real desire to understand the man and his world and his work and to try without being too literal to find the theatrical equivalent for this fictional world, to match the integrity of the original.

In the case of *Tomorrow*, my approach to dramatizing it was, in all candor, something that I stumbled on. Over the years, I have grown in my appreciation of the basic mythic quality of the story. A critic named Eric Bentley said that he feels *Tomorrow* is the nearest thing to Greek tragedy he's ever seen in films. I was just bowled over by that kind of reaction. And many people have reacted to the film in this way. I can only tell you that I, as a person, never ask myself anything but one question, and that is: "How do *I* feel about it?" I did not necessarily go out to create a tragic character. What interested me was to explore the relationship between Fentry and the woman. I understand, though I never met him, that Faulkner was very pleased with this.

I think Hollywood has so often failed with Faulkner because they insisted on improving him, for whatever reasons: trying to make him more palatable, more popular, more commercial. I think it would be well for any dramatist to give up this approach. Faulkner can be dramatized. He can't be improved.

DECLARATION OF INDEPENDENTS
Gilbert Pearlman and Paul Roebling

PEARLMAN   Our connection with the film began when we saw Herbert Berghof's stage production on opening night. I saw two magnificent performances by Bob Duvall and Olga Bellin and that was the basis of my enthusiasm for putting it on film.

ROEBLING   When I saw the play, I said, "God, that's a movie. That could be the most stunningly beautiful movie of a Faulkner work that's ever been done."

PEARLMAN   Paul and Olga and I talked about it that same night over a few drinks. What excited me about the work was the basic human relationships among all the characters, something I had missed a lot in recent films and plays. Then some time passed and I guess neither Paul nor I could get the work out of our minds. We talked again and agreed that if we both thought it would make a hell of a film, why shouldn't we do it. I contacted Horton's agent, Lucy Kroll, who at that time was my agent and that began it.

ROEBLING   Gilbert had written a play which Berghof had staged a while back at his studio that I wanted to do as a film, and we had talked for some time about the two of us starting a film company. Well, here we now had two properties. We agreed we would do the Faulkner work first, thinking it would be a great send-off for us and more attractive in terms of getting financial backing and distribution.

PEARLMAN   We were pretty relaxed about the casting because our two major roles were already cast.

ROEBLING   I had had a good working experience with Joe Anthony who directed the film. He directed "The Lark" in 1955, a play about Joan of Arc by Jean Anouilh, starring Julie Harris, in which I played The Dauphin. And I was familiar with his other work as a director, both on stage and in film. I really felt that Joe had a great feeling for simple people and simple circumstances and what he did in *Tomorrow* proved me right.

PEARLMAN   After Horton finished the script, our next goal was raising the money. Paul put up $50,000 front money which kept us going for a year in preproduction. I assembled a crew. But I also spent a lot of time trying to raise the money for production on the basis of the script and was totally unsuccessful.

ROEBLING   We went to all the major distributors, some owners of movie chains, bankers, private persons, everybody we thought would be interested. We gave out scripts. Everyone had a direct, immediate and wonderfully generous response to the script. And they would all be very excited by the fact that we had a William Faulkner story for $20,000 and a Horton Foote script for $20,000. But the minute they heard that it was going to be shot in black and white, and with two unknowns, Olga Bellin and Robert Duvall, in the lead that was the end of the deal. (*The Godfather* hadn't come out yet and even that didn't make a bankable name for Bob.) Everybody wanted something other than what we were talking about in order to get the money. They all wanted color and most of them wanted Jennifer Jones or somebody else like her to play the lead.

PEARLMAN   Even after we went into production and had an hour of the film put together so that they could see the performances by Bob and Olga, still no takers. And even after the film was completely finished, the music scored and everything, we showed it around to all of the major companies and again they all said the same thing: "This is artistically beautiful but we don't see it as commercial." Except one man. Peter Meyers of 20th Century-Fox. He adored the film and tried to convince not only the top executives of his own company to pick it up but also tried to sell it to other major distributors. No takers. The cost of bringing in the negative was $435,000. It was entirely paid for by Paul Roebling. And the money for distribution and promotion, another $200,000, also came from Paul. We paid our cast members, except the two principals, Screen Actors Guild scale; we made percentage arrangements with Bob, Olga, Horton, and Joe.

ROEBLING   Unfortunately, the film did not make money. Not one cent. I had to sell and mortgage houses and stocks and other things I owned and it took me several years to get out of hock. But I couldn't have done the film any other way. Certainly not the way those who might have put up the money wanted it done. I believe we could have gotten backing, most of it or even all of it, if we had agreed to do it in color instead of black and white.

Everybody wanted me to shoot it in color and then produce some black and white prints for the theaters and do a color rendition for television so that the rights could be presold for television and then I would have had distribution deals up front. However, I don't know if you've ever seen a black and white print produced from a color negative. It is not what one would call professional quality. So in nixing that idea I really nixed the financial viability of the film.

What very few people understood about the movie—and even those who were really excited with the notion of filming a Faulkner work—was that the choice for color is the choice for style. They mistook the movie for a realistic film. It isn't at all. Faulkner writes in essences of character. *Tomorrow* as a film is a style piece. The characters were essences of people behaving; man, as a hero of the earth, able to endure tomorrow and tomorrow and tomorrow. Faulkner didn't write in realistic terms in this work. He was terribly stylistic, I felt. He brought out the essence of what he saw in these people. His work had what Horton Foote called a mythic quality. And

Horton kept that mythic quality in his script. And, of course, we were going to keep it in the production of the film. It had to be done in black and white. *The Reivers*, on the other hand, should have been done in color. It was like a musical comedy and that was the way Faulkner wrote it. I never would have done *Tomorrow*, no matter how richly I had been tempted, in anything but black and white.

PEARLMAN   I might add that the black and white thing came up again when just a few years ago we tried to sell the film to television. All the networks dismissed it out of hand because it wasn't in color.

ROEBLING   You can see that what we had here was a low-budget film. And we had a low-budget shooting schedule. First of all, there was six months of preproduction in Tupelo, Mississippi, which I did together with one assistant and the production manager's assistant. The three of us were down there collecting the props, getting the locations wrapped up, having the set built, getting the local people together who were going to be in the film. Everyone wanted to shoot the movie in New Hampshire. But I said, "No, this is going to be shot where Faulkner intended it to be put." This story was about people with an unmistakable quality of their own. And you've got to go down there and make use of the terrain and capture what these people are like physically, how one must be to live physically as these people did without a totally balanced diet in this hard, rough hill country where they depended on the earth and cotton for their survival.

Everybody in the cast, except for the central characters, was local. I don't think anybody could have been better than that preacher. He was really a preacher. The shopkeeper was really a shopkeeper. The child who played young Jackson and Longstreet was the son of a local farmer.

The shots outside of the cabin were filmed at a sawmill in Itawamba County, Mississippi, and about twenty-five miles from Faulkner's birthplace. I brought a building in from another county and placed it on the sawmill grounds; I don't think my back has ever been the same.

Joe Anthony, the director, found the courthouse we used in a little deserted Mississippi town called Jacinto in Alcorn

County. There was not a great problem here about blocking things off. It really was pretty much just what you saw there. It's an historic structure, but I was a little disappointed that it didn't have the dome, and the cupola and the pillars—the trademarks of the Southern courthouse.

We built a set for the interior of the cabin in the Tupelo fairgrounds building. The town was so happy to have a movie done there that they built us a soundproof wall around it at their expense. We were sitting in the middle of a railroad yard, and adjustments had to be made on our microphone so that everytime a train went by we weren't all blown out of the sound box. As nice as the soundproof wall was, it wasn't like being in MGM Studio 45 by any means. This problem accounts for the hollowness of some of our sound.

A week before we went into shooting we did not have a director of photography. They sent me down a film from CBS in New York which had been shot about a black child in the slums of the city, and I detected some great sensitivity in the close-up shots and some of the surroundings. I said, "Gee, this man looks good." So we went with it. The first day I met him I said, "Look, I'm really sorry this has been such short notice but I have been looking all over America for the man, whom you may know, who shot "Jazz on a Summer's Day," the documentary about the Newport Jazz Festival. And he said, "Yes, I shot it." It was one of those psychic phenomena that take place. That's how we got Alan Green.

PEARLMAN   We shot the film in two sessions. The first session in the spring of 1970 was a six-week shoot with a standard I.A. union film crew of thirty people. Even though we had several scenes yet to shoot, we disbanded at the end of exactly six weeks and went back to New York for a very simple reason: We ran out of money.

ROEBLING   When we got back to New York, we discovered that the very last sequence we shot before we left, with the boy and Fentry in the cotton field was destroyed in the lab. We told the insurance company that to set up a cotton field in the North, which is what MGM would have done, would have cost $75,000. We received $6,000 out of a $40,000 claim. So with that and more money that I put in, we went back in September for another five days of shooting. This time, instead of a crew of thirty, we had five men and Joe Anthony, the cinematographer, Alan Green, Bob Duvall, and myself. And in those five days we shot one-third as much footage as we had shot in six weeks with a thirty-man crew. A most amazing week of shooting. All in all, when we went into the editing we had a film more than four hours long.

We were practically 18 months in the editing. Whole chunks had to simply come out of the film and that left us still with four hours. We got it down to two hours and we still knew it was too long. We always felt that as good as the film was, what was going on was too fragile to hold an audience's attention for that length of time. No one was burning down Atlanta.

Then, Joe had in a way not wanted the film we ended with, until he saw the film. He had wanted the relationship between the man and the woman expanded. That to him was the whole movie. Basically, I saw the story as being about a miscarriage of justice, both in the courtroom and out in the world where this woman dies as a result of injustices. This was what Mr. Faulkner wrote and this was what I wanted to put on the screen. So actually what happened was, Reva and Horton and Gil and I took what film footage we had and created the ending, the montage of the boy growing up and the court-house ending.

PEARLMAN   When we had the film ready for distribution and—we cut it to 102 minutes—still nobody would take it on. Paul and I handled it ourselves, opening it in New York at the 68th Street Playhouse, a small art theater. Our strategy was to get good reviews and a long run at the Playhouse, say for several months to close to a year. That would bring the major distributors back to us and might result in one of them handling national distribution. We got all splendid reviews except from Vincent Canby of *The New York Times*. But if you don't get the *Times* in an art theater, you don't get your audience. And if you don't get a long run, you don't get the distributors. We ran at the 68th Street Playhouse for eight weeks. Interestingly enough, we were on every "Ten Best" list of consequence for that year (1972) except the *Times*. After the New

York run, we turned over the distribution to a new organization of young men who tried hard but were not too experienced in dealing with exhibitors. And even though in some places we had a pretty good run, the bad drove out the good, and our film was exhibited out of all the money we could give to it.

ROEBLING   The experience of this film was a little disillusioning. I was and still am saddened by the fact that people did not want to see the movie enough that it could at least break even. But I feel that we did what we set out to do: To make the most faithful rendition of Faulkner that had ever been put on the screen. I believe the film is going to make money though. Someday. We all have hopes.

PEARLMAN   I wouldn't have traded the experience for anything. Yet I don't think I could go through the experience again, because to produce a film independently takes so much energy and is so exhausting and so much of the time is spent banging your head against the wall.

ROEBLING   I think that everybody concerned with the production, the author, director, cinematographer, editor, actors, the crew, and the producers, performed with great integrity. In addition, this film offers Robert Duvall in what was one of the most stunning performances I have ever seen in my life.

YOU MUST DRAW FROM WITHIN YOURSELF
Robert Duvall

I STILL POINT to Fentry as my favorite part. It was my most complete film role, certainly the most complete up until, and still on a par with, Santini in *The Great Santini* (released in 1980). When Herbert Berghof gave me Horton Foote's play that had been done on television and said he wanted to do it as a stage piece in his studio, I figured I would go ahead and do it with him, as an exercise, you know, and nothing more would come of it. But I started to read it and couldn't put it down. I hadn't read the Faulkner story, in fact I didn't read it until after I made the movie. Horton had put in much of his own material and it was great. He knows the area and the people.

Herbert changed it from the way it was done on TV. In order to compress time, he had flashbacks and in that way overcame the inability of a stage play to jump around in time. The lawyer was the narrator and this allowed me to step in and out of time, from the past to the present and back again, I could play Fentry older or younger with the narrator setting the time and place, without the curtain going down.

One of the differences between playing the role on stage and in film was in playing the interiors, in the cabin and so forth; so much of Fentry's story took place in the cabin. I feel that interior scenes usually work better on stage. That's not so much because of place but because on stage you get a good run out of it and you do it every night and you can build on it and work on it and you have a continuity of emotion. And you can relate with and work off the audience. Like one night in doing the play, the rain was coming down and we heard it on the roof of the theater and we listened to it and we played off of it. And another night, an eight-year-old boy sitting in the second row was so involved in the play, he was crying. And we played off that. On the stage the audience is there and you can use them.

But no matter where you're doing it, on stage, TV, or film, acting a character is something you detect rather than see. In acting, you must remember it's always you doing it, you must draw from within yourself. I try to find things that are different from what's in the script, different stimuli. But, of course, it's got to be there within you before it can come out. I don't want to act the part, I want to be the part.

Doing the play on stage influenced and shaped the character for me. The roots of Fentry, especially the way he spoke, came to me from an experience I had when I was a senior in high school in St. Louis. I once went with my brother to southern Missouri to spend a few days, and went into Arkansas and we met this guy. He didn't open his mouth until he had something to say; he talked straightforward. He talked like a cow. Fentry was such a guy, a closed guy. He was no retard; he was a simple man and I wanted to keep him that way. I wanted him to be a stoic. One night during the play, Fentry was moved to tears in one scene. I didn't hold back the tears but I turned my back to the audience. I didn't want them to see him show that emotion. Fentry was such an inside person, whatever was happening to him, he kept to himself. I wanted him to open up only when he was with the small boy. After all, look at the circumstances Fentry lived in: no women in the family; he was alone most of the time, out in the fields working alone, taking care of the lumber camp in the winter when nobody was using it, living in the cabin alone, eating alone, sleeping alone. And most of the action took place in 1905 in Mississippi where working the land was hard and was in the middle of nowhere. He was the exact opposite of the character of Eddie Carbone, the part I played in Arthur Miller's *A View From the Bridge*. Eddie was articulate, he had to have everything he felt come out. Of course, Fentry was a great challenge to me as an actor, to keep him this inside person and yet show the audience what was going on within him.

When I got to the film and we went down to Mississippi to shoot it, I drove around and walked around and listened to the people talk. I didn't make tapes. I didn't want to imitate, I wanted to absorb, you know. I found that most of the Southern accents were somewhat high pitched and nasal. But when I went deeper into the region, into the more remote areas where Fentry would have lived, the voices became deeper and more in the throat. I found that my original inspiration, the cow-talking guy in Arkansas, still held up. I used it in the film. And I found that those people who objected to Fentry's dialect were usually people who had never been anywhere in the South, and certainly had never been in the deep South, in Faulkner's country.

I didn't see the final print of *Tomorrow* before it was shown. In fact, I didn't see the film until a year or so after I finished working on it. It turned out to be a good film, even a great film, but it was inferior to what it should have been. I have to say I was stunned when I saw it. They had cut out the scenes I did with the boy after he grew up. In my opinion, the audience had to see Fentry see the boy grow up, and then

Fentry's decision not to acquit the man who killed the boy would have more meaning, make more sense. As I say, it was a wonderful picture and a great part for me, but I think it could have been a greater movie. I've got to say, too, that I was dissatisfied with the handling of the film, the distribution, or really, how it wasn't distributed, how it was ignored all the way through Hollywood. And shooting it as independent film, we didn't have the advantages of the studios, we didn't have the money and time to shoot all the scenes that needed to be shot. And reshot. And I can't help but wonder how this movie would have turned out had it been done by Hollywood all the way.

ON PLAYING SARAH
Olga Bellin

I WAS DRAWN into the part by the kind of woman Sarah was and what she was seeking. I always thought of it as a great love story. To me, Sarah was above all a woman who had been rejected in life, disappointed in what life had to offer her. And then she met Fentry who was offering what she had never experienced before: true, unselfish love. I thought of Sarah first as a woman, and her responses and reactions to what happened to her were the same as any woman's would have been no matter where she was from. But, of course, the authenticity of her as a native of Mississippi was important if she was to be believable. My one preparation, not being a Southerner, was the dialect. I spent a good deal of time down there where we were working on the film, just trying to walk around the streets and be taken for a Mississippian. I would walk around there and see how well I could fit in and be accepted and not be recognized as being a Northerner. When people didn't know I was with the film company, I did pretty well.

But Duvall, of course, worked in his own way on his dialect. His manner of speech was different from mine. He had his own rhythms. He was from a different county in Mississippi and our characters were different. Sarah was a woman who was very garrulous and Fentry was not able to talk. In the beginning that made for an awkward relationship between us and our different speech patterns showed that. And as we got more used to each other, and as the love story unfolded, the way we each would speak together would enhance that relationship. In Fentry's case, at first he seemed to speak in a monotone; he wasn't used to talking to anyone, having lived so long alone in that cabin. But as Sarah and Fentry grew closer, and he had reason to speak and he wanted to speak, his speech had inflections he didn't have before. His inflections increased. And Sarah, you might say, went the other way. As she grew more comfortable with Fentry, more safe and secure—feelings she had never had before—her speech became softer, less compulsive.

Both Bob and I were helped in the film by having done the play at the Berghof studio where it was done in a very intimate way. We didn't go in for histrionics; we didn't have to project to the second balcony. So when we finally got in front of the cameras, our relationship was not a great deal different. But what was different and wonderful was to be surrounded by reality. All the things you had to work for as an actor on the stage were just given to you in doing the film. It was wonderful actually to be in a room, to go outside, to open a door that was really a door, to see the sun and the grass, to look at the land, to touch and even smell what you were talking about. This was so inspiring especially for this story where place is so important. To actually have the cotton in the field, to walk on the site where Fentry is going to build the house, to really feel the cold wind on your face and hear it blow was just marvelous and invaluable to me as a performer.

And I've got to say how supportive the others were in the film. For instance, Sudie Bond who played Mrs. Hulie, the midwife, in the birth scene, a scene that was in the film and not in any of the other versions. The way Joe Anthony shot the scene, just letting the two of us go through it was most helpful. I truly felt as if Sudie, who is a Kentucky girl originally, was a midwife and had done this over and over again. And what she did was to get on with it and let me bite the cloth and hold on to my hands and urge me to push and do whatever had to be done. We weren't doing a scene for a film as much as going through an experience, and it was edited later into the film and put into its proper place and tempo.

DIRECTING: TO REVEAL THE BEHAVIOR OF PEOPLE
Joseph Anthony

MY PREVIOUS connection with Faulkner was nothing more than as a natural reader of his works, not as a student, but as an admirer. I had not read "Tomorrow" as a short story, nor had I seen the TV play. I had seen the stage play at Herbert Berghof's studio and admired the work very much. It was beautifully done. So honest. Horton Foote is an ancient chum of mine. We were young actors together and had kept in touch through the years on both a professional and personal basis. I had known Olga Bellin as a splendid actress and had directed Paul Roebling on Broadway in *The Lark*. And so I went into the film with a profound love of the work and a feeling that all of us in the production had a long and established creative respect for each other.

Yet, in studying the script I realized very early that we could be confounded by a basic matter of dramaturgy. I don't think Faulkner is particularly cinematic; his chief interest is theme and that is not easy to dramatize. And in Horton's script, if you notice, there is no dramatic conflict. There is a problem, but not a conflict. I mean, if Sarah had to leave Fentry's cabin, Fentry would do nothing to keep her there, even though his yearning would be for this companionship.

Horton's great talent is his ear. It is still a mystery to me how Horton was able to invent dialogue, yet give the impression that these were monosyllabic people. He knows how people talk, especially Southerners, and in this play his conversations—and his silences—between people reveal their natures, their relationships. Their conversations are of a revelatory nature rather than dramatic. So that with these two people—Fentry and Sarah—the dramatic conflict is really their getting to know each other. But I felt that Horton's revelatory dialogue had value, particularly in cinematic terms. It drew you into the nature of these people, which, particularly for myself, being a northerner, is of dramatic value, because we are not familiar with people who possess such willingness to yield to silence, to slow development of communicative exchange. Those qualities are getting lost in our rapid-paced world. Those qualities are being denied in our appetite to show off, to entertain each other in conversation, to disturb each other almost like debaters and constantly contend with each other. Not necessarily to say anything meaningful to each other, but using noise to keep us in contact. But in this film we have a beautiful, basic, primitive need of human beings to communicate.

Well, as you can see, I had some problems as a director. There was the matter of Hollywood, where the conventional wisdom pushes everybody to rush to get to the next event, to play on that which jazzes up the events of life and usually clouds its value, its meaning. But because Horton, and Paul Roebling, and Gilbert Pearlman, and Olga Bellin and Bob Duvall, and Alan Green, our cameraman, and Reva Schlesinger, our editor, are such human beings of integrity, we didn't go Hollywood.

Our main problem all the way through was that of selection. We had four hours plus of story on film. What happened all the way through, when we cut it to three hours, to two hours, to its final form, was our selecting out all the material, and keeping only that which was truly relevant to the basic story: the meeting of Sarah and Fentry, the development of their relationship; their love of each other, their mutual protection and aid as human beings; and the loss of each other, that barrenness of two lonely human beings not much wanted by anyone, being deprived of the person they love both by death and then later by the young boy being torn from the foster father.

Throughout the whole process of filming and editing, Paul, Horton, and I had only one conflict: how to use the narrators such as the neighbors and the young lawyer. Both Horton and Paul are very loyal to Faulkner and that loyalty made problems for me as a director. The essential technique by which the story is uncovered through the lawyer is a narrative form that Faulkner could use as a short story writer, but it serves no purpose cinematically. In an effort to try to include these narrative characters in the film we spent a great deal of time shooting material that I knew from the beginning would not be useful. But we had such a camaraderie and respect for each other, that, from my point of view, I just said, "No, this must be done the way all three of us can please each other in doing it."

In the editing room we found that we needed these narrators less and less. They became distractions and took the blossom off the play. Cinematically we were served by sticking to the story of how these two people communicated with each other, their need to communicate, and what happened as a result. When you tell that story, you answer the mystery question of why Fentry will not free the man who killed the young boy.

I have the greatest belief that one of the things a motion picture must do is this: it must reveal the behavior of people, how people reveal themselves through what they do and how they do it. I think we accomplished that in this film. And I like to think that was my contribution, my only true gift, to the film. For instance, the sugar candy Fentry gives Sarah. That's Horton, it wasn't in Faulkner's story. Well, that whole scene and the whole business about Christmas tells more about Sarah, about her past, and who she is, and the kind of person she is, than anything she could have told about herself. And when the father takes the baby in, without a question, that tells all about him and his relationship with his son, Fentry.

One of the vital decisions about this film was, of course, to shoot it in black and white. That was, I'm happy to say, a common feeling among all of us. First of all, even today, color is still not true. And then, too, it makes things beautiful in a commonplace way. We felt that color would be apt to sentimentalize the story, to pretty it up. This picture shouldn't be sentimental and it should have its own beauty. Color has an automatic built-in contrast value. It's so much easier to make a picture that you can see. That's why amateurs like color, because the color comes out better. It's much harder to get true contrast and true definition and true revelation of moments of truth in black and white than it is in color.

And another thing, we were all, of course, nuts for

Walker Evans. [The photographer famous for photos of the South taken during the Great Depression in the 1930s] I was so glad that Alan Green, our cameraman, felt the same way. Before he came on the picture I challenged him because most of the work he showed me was color. I said, "Wait a minute. We all want to do this in black and white." And he said, "I can't tell you how I long to do a black and white film because that will mean I'll have to work my tail off." We wanted a grey movie, not harsh black and white, and to get contrast in grey is very difficult. But that's what we wanted, that's what Alan Green went for, and that's what he gave us.

One thing about this film that people who like it always comment on is its universality. To me, the universality of its theme is the meat of it, the power of it. The specific quality about the South is only color to me. The accents, the cotton fields, the wind, and the sawmill give it an authentic flavor. But if it were only a local portrait, it would not be as significant a piece of film literature. The film is a reminder for humankind everywhere about primitive, basic needs and the wonderful quality of human beings who can endure under degradation and still remain magnificent and unique.

Of course, we tried for truth in every detail. And that's where Paul Roebling was so great. Very often the role of the producer is the obsession with having a hit, and certainly Paul and Gil wanted a film that would make money. Their other main job was to see that the clock doesn't become an enemy of the work process. You know, it's mostly those external things that can prevent a work from being well-realized. But Paul, in addition to his regular producing duties of supervising money, schedules, and union crews, had an obsession for the right props and costumes and everything else that would be seen by the camera. A great burden was taken off my back because of Paul's extraordinary, concentrated, purposeful determination that everything be authentic.

Because we were a low-budget production and because everything connected with it was so dedicated and in tune, my style of directing seemed to fit in nicely. First of all, I have to say that I do not like to show off as a director. I can't stand it when the camera is played around with and gets in the way or calls attention to itself. So I prepare considerably for what I want the camera to do. I don't overshoot. If anything, I go in the other direction. And Alan Green, having been so busy in commercial movies for television, was very pleased to wield a sensitive camera that didn't move unless it was essential and added to the scene. The camera work had to be very simple and its main purpose was to show the audience what it needed to see. But I certainly took suggestions when we came on the set for shooting. I don't like an atmosphere on a set of conflict. I'm not one of those who believe that actors perform better if you get them all upset, that it gives them energy. I like to work in harmony, so if someone has an idea and I see that the clock is not going to defeat us, I do it, and let it prove itself in the editing room.

The leading actors had already found the play with Herbert Berghof, so I worked to keep their performance as true as they had been in the theater. While Olga gave a fine performance, Duvall displayed an extraordinary gift of identity, that is of great depth and stature. I think Duvall's portrait in terms of acting is unique in all of American and English-speaking motion picture-making. Few past performers have had the economy of that acting performance, that depth of identity. I'm glad this film is finally getting an audience.

EDITING A LOVED ONE

Reva Schlesinger

EDITING this film took a very long time; we were on it over a year. I started with them when they were down in Mississippi for the first six weeks of shooting. I didn't go down there, I stayed in New York cutting the material coming up from location. Then, there was a hiatus over the summer, after which they went down for five days and sent a lot of stuff back and when that was over we started. My first cut was four and a half hours.

In the beginning, Joe Anthony and I would screen the material together and Joe would give me his general feelings about what he thought was important in the scene and how he thought it should be handled. And then I would go off and work on it by myself. Many directors want to be in the cutting room all the time, but I prefer to work alone. I think most cutters do. Fortunately, on this film I was allowed to do it that way. Then, Joe and Paul and Gil would come in to screen what I had done, and we'd talk about it, make changes and then show it to them. One thing about this film is that we all had similar feelings about the material. I think this feeling comes through in the film.

Our big problem, of course, was that we had a tremendous amount of material that we all loved so dearly that had to go. There were, for instance, several scenes about Sarah's background, and Fentry coming to the sawmill, and the way the sawmill operated; and especially after Sarah's burial, a long sequence with Fentry coming back to her grave and then going to the place where he was going to build their house— they were lovely scenes, and cutting them out became a ruthless thing. But necessary. It's like cutting off a leg or an arm of a loved one. But you've got to get the film into some sort of shape so that it can run in a theater.

I didn't see the TV play and I hadn't read Faulkner's story until after I got into the cutting of the film. But I loved the material on film the minute I saw it. It was so sensitive. I knew it had to be played and therefore edited as a very delicate graphic of people who are inarticulate, but who have very deep feelings and an intense capacity for giving love. What they couldn't express verbally we had to show on the screen.

In this film, as in just about every feature film, you start with the script. But then, so often, what's written on the page changes when it's shot. You know the actor gives it a new shading, the director sees it on the set a different way. When you're out in the field shooting, you use the script as a springboard and so when it comes back to me in the editing room, I take the script and make it conform to the shot material. For example, I think Joe shot the love story part magnificently. He let the relationship between Sarah and Fentry come through; he gave them time. No script writer could predict what Bob Duvall can do with a scene. I think he has in this film such controlled violence. I don't mean in the sense of shooting somebody, but I mean emotional violence. There's such a passion there and as Fentry he sits on it so tightly that even though he's not saying very much and he's not doing much overt acting, it comes through. I mean, your eye is riveted on him all the time. And what Joe has to do as a director and I have to do in the cutting is to make sure to let all that love between Sarah and Fentry come through.

You know you can do millions of things in the cutting room, but you can't do what you don't have on film. I can give you one scene that took an exceptional amount of work, and one that Joe Anthony said really had to be made in the cutting room. The birth of Sarah's baby. What Joe really shot there was a long roll of Sarah just thrashing around—the close-ups of her head and her crying out, and the only connecting material was the shots of the midwife pushing down and the longer shots of Sarah. And what you saw in that scene was all of those close-ups of Sarah cut together showing the pain and intensity of what she was going through. Here was one instance where my documentary background helped. In documentaries, you get what you can and make up your story later. The birth scene wasn't written as such in the script and Joe didn't say to me, "Do it this way, do it that way." But I think among all of us, the thought of the scene was there. I did it that way and nobody touched it. That's what a cutter loves.

The end of the film was made in the cutting room.

Joe Anthony had shot material for an ending with Fentry and the grown-up boy, Buck. Well, you see, we used local people for a lot of the parts, like the preacher, who turned out to be simply marvelous. But the boy he chose for Buck just didn't have it; it came out so poor in comparison with the quality of everything else, we couldn't use it. So, we had to go for another ending. But I didn't do it myself. We all sat down and faced the problem together. There was no money the way there usually is in Hollywood. We couldn't say, "Well, we'll just go out and shoot what we need. Wouldn't it be great if we had this or that?" We had to go with what we had, and so cooperatively we tried things, talked about things, and finally agreed on what we could do and we went ahead with it.

When it came to the music everyone agreed that the score should be very simple, in keeping with both the story and the character of Fentry. We wanted nothing sophisticated in its treatment with a minimum of instrumentation. The composer, Irwin Stahl, gave us a basic idea of his themes on the piano, and then certain scenes were agreed on for scoring. However, and this is very often the case, when we got back to the cutting room after the music was recorded and tried sections out, we found that sometimes a piece of music originally meant for one scene seemed to work in unexpected ways when laid in against a scene not planned for that music. Sometimes, even though what seemed excellent music was recorded, it turned out that silence was best. That is what is so fascinating about the film process: the experimentation and the excitement of discovery.

I particularly recall one example. A sad refrain, simply sung, was cut into the sound tracts to be tried in the very last scene of the film when Fentry rides past the camera and into the distance. At the final mix, the music seemed most moving against the image. But, when just to see how it would be, the music was left out, it was clear that Fentry, riding off alone, in absolute silence, was a great deal more moving. And so, the final scene remained as it now is.

You know, I have found that even all of these years later, everybody who sees the film loves it. It's gratifying. But it's also terrible that it doesn't get seen because of the distribution set up in the industry. There's so much in it of quality. The major studios made their decisions on whether they could sell it, on the fact that they couldn't promote a black-and-white film. Those of us who made the film made all of the decisions on the aesthetics of the film. So that was the problem. But I still think that the film has its audience.

NOTES ON THE FILM'S CREATORS

HORTON FOOTE left his native Texas to study acting at the Pasadena Community Playhouse and was later a member of the American Actors Company in New York. He has written plays, screenplays and television plays including "The Trip to Bountiful," "The Chase," "The Traveling Lady," and "Baby, the Rain Must Fall." His work reveals a deep and abiding familiarity with Southern places and people. He received the Academy Award for Best Screenplay for both *To Kill a Mockingbird* and *Tender Mercies*. In addition to "Tomorrow," Foote has written television adaptations for two other Faulkner stories, "Old Man" and "Barn Burning." "Old Man" was a highly-praised Playhouse 90 production in 1958. "Barn Burning," broadcast in 1980, was an outstanding entry on the acclaimed PBS series, The American Short Story. Foote is the author of *The Orphan's Home,* a cycle of nine plays, three of which— *Courtship, Valentine's Day,* and *1918*—have been produced by the HB Playwrights Foundation in New York City.

GILBERT PEARLMAN left his native Iowa in the early 1950s to pursue graduate studies in New York at Columbia University, where he studied playwriting with the late John Gassner. In 1959, he began teaching playwriting at the Uta Hagen–Herbert Berghof Studio. A year later he adapted Ugo Betti's "The Queen and The Rebels" for a production which starred Miss Hagen and was directed by Mr. Berghof. Concurrent with that activity, he worked in advertising for Walt Disney Productions and Columbia Pictures. In 1964, with Miss Hagen and Mr. Berghof, he founded the HB Playwrights Foundation in Greenwich Village and was its artistic director for two years. In 1969, he formed Filmgroup Productions with Paul Roebling. He is now a partner in the New York advertising firm of Pearlman/Rowe/Kolomatsky, Inc.

PAUL ROEBLING has spent the better part of the last 30 years as an actor on the New York stage. His appearance in a Broadway production of Pearl Buck's *The Desert Incident* earned for him a Theater World Award. In another Broadway role, he portrayed the Dauphin to Julie Harris's St. Joan in *The Lark* under the direction of Joseph Anthony. In 1962 he won Off-Broadway's coveted Obie Award for his starring role in the dramatization of F. Scott Fitzgerald's first novel, *This Side of Paradise*. Mr. Roebling has appeared on a number of television specials including Hallmark Hall of Fame's presentation of "Anastasia", in which he played opposite Lynn Fontanne and Julie Harris. In the 1950s he coproduced with Theresa Hayden, an Off-Broadway cycle of plays that featured such prominent stars as Eli Wallach and Patricia Neal. After coproducing *Tomorrow* Mr. Roebling returned to acting. He has since completed "Brooklyn Bridge," a television documentary for WNET; and three films, *Prince of the City, Blue Thunder,* and *The End of August.*

ROBERT DUVALL began his film career in 1963 with his appearance in the award-winning adaptation of *To Kill a Mockingbird,* in which he played the mysterious recluse, Boo Radley. Then, Duvall went on to excel as the religious fanatic, Major Burns, in M*A*S*H and the lecherous cop in *The Rain People*. The actor's portrayal of Hagen, the WASP lawyer in *The Godfather,* won him an Oscar nomination, as did his depiction of the outrageous Lieutenant Colonel Kilgore in Francis Coppola's prize-winning *Apocalypse, Now.* Since his appearance in *Tomorrow,* Duvall has added numerous character portraits, as well as leading roles, to his credit. He played the icy TV hatchet-man in *Network,* and in *The Great Santini,* Duvall took a leading role as Bull Meechum, a spit-and-polish Marine pilot. He received an Academy Award for best actor for his performance as a down-and-out country singer in the Horton Foote film, *Tender Mercies.* Duvall has shown that he is more than a versatile actor. He directed *We're Not the Jet Set,* a documentary about a Nebraska rodeo family and *Angelo, My Love,* a film about gypsies in New York City.

OLGA BELLIN began her acting career as a teenage "wunderkind" of midwestern stock companies. After graduating Phi Beta Kappa from Northwestern University she continued her study and work with Uta Hagen and Herbert Berghof in New York. She played opposite Miss Hagen in both the stage and television versions of "A Month in the Country," for which she earned the Theater World Award. Miss Bellin is especially remembered on Broadway for her role as Paul Scofield's daughter Margaret in the hit, *A Man for All Seasons.* During the "Golden Age" of TV drama she took leading parts in Philco, Studio One, Kraft Theater, and Westinghouse productions. She played the lead in Horton Foote's stage version of *The Travelling Lady,* while working as an understudy for the actress Kim Stanley. In 1984 she opened in New York in *Zelda* by William Luce. The play, directed by her husband Paul Roeblin, is a solo performance based on the writing of Zelda Fitzgerald.

JOSEPH ANTHONY is known both as an actor and director. He made his New York stage debut as an actor in 1937 and as a director in 1948. He has since directed numerous plays including *Bullfight, Winesburg, Ohio, Under the Yum-Yum Tree,* and *The Homecoming.* He appeared regularly in dramatic television programs from 1947–54 and directed television episodes of *Profiles in Courage.* He has directed the following films: *The Rainmaker, The Matchmaker, Career, All in a Night's Work,* and *Captive City.* He has taught theatre arts at Vassar College, Hunter College, and New York University.

REVA SCHLESINGER, the film editor of *Tomorrow,* has spent a large part of her career editing documentaries for industries such as the Ford Motor Co. and U.S. Steel. She has tackled a diverse range of subjects: from "Head Start Child-of-the-Year" for the U.S. Government to "Michelangelo" for Time-Life, Inc., for which she wrote the script. She has also worked in the complex role of writer/coproducer/director/editor for several films, including *Once there Was a City.* One of these, *Rembrandt: A Self-Portrait,* was nominated for an Academy Award as best short of the year. *Sweet Love/Bitter,* a feature film produced independently in 1966, is another of her many editing credits. She lives in Nantucket, Massachusetts.

FAULKNER: A TELEVISION AND FILM CHECKLIST

TELEVISION ADAPTATIONS
"The Brooch," NBC Lux Video Theater, 1953
"Shall Not Perish," NBC Lux Video Theater, 1954
"Barn Burning," CBS Suspense, 1954.
"Smoke," CBS Suspense, 1954.
"Old Man," CBS Playhouse 90, 1958.
"Tomorrow," CBS Playhouse 90, 1960.
"Barn Burning," PBS The American Short Story Series, 1980.

FILM ADAPTATIONS
The Story of Temple Drake, Paramount, 1933, adapted from *Sanctuary.*
Intruder in the Dust, MGM, 1951.
The Tarnished Angels, Universal, 1957, adapted from *Pylon.*
The Long Hot Summer, Twentieth Century-Fox, 1960, adapted from *The Hamlet.*
The Sound and the Fury, Twentieth Century-Fox, 1959.
Sanctuary, Twentieth Century-Fox, 1961.
The Reivers, Warner Brothers, 1970.
Tomorrow, Filmgroup, 1972.

SELECTED BIBLIOGRAPHY

Arnheim, Rudolph. *Film as Art*, University of California Press, 1957.

Averson, Richard and White, David Manning. (Editors) *Electronic Drama*, Beacon, 1971.

―――. *Sight, Sound, and Society, Motion Pictures and Television in America*, Beacon, 1968.

Barnouw, Eric. *The Image Empire*, Oxford Press, 1970.

Bazin, André. *What is Cinema*, University of California Press, 1967.

Beaver, Frank E. *On Film*, McGraw-Hill, 1983.

Beja, Morris. *Film and Literature, An Introduction*, Longman, 1979.

Bluestone, George. *Novels into Film*, The Johns Hopkins Press, 1957.

Bobker, Lee R. *Elements of FIlm*, Harcourt, Brace & World, 1969.

Bradford, M. E. "Faulkner's 'Tomorrow' and the Plain People," *Studies in Short Fiction*, 1965.

Brownlow, Kevin. *Hollywood: The Pioneers*, Knopf, 1979.

―――. *The Parade's Gone By*, Knopf, 1968.

Capra, Frank. *The Name Above the Title*, Macmillan, 1971.

Chayefsky, Paddy. *Television Plays*, Simon and Schuster, 1955.

Emmons, Carol A. *Short Stories on Film*, Libraries Unlimited, 1978.

Enser, A. G. S. *Filmed Books and Plays*, Seminar Press, 1971.

Foote, Horton. *Three Plays*, Harcourt, Brace & World, Inc., 1962.

Geduld, Harry M. (Editor) *Film Makers on Film Making*, Indiana University Press, 1967.

Gessner, Robert. *The Moving Image*, E. P. Dutton & Co., 1968.

Giannetti, Louis. *Masters of the American Cinema*, Prentice Hall, 1981.

Harrington, Evans and Abadie, Ann J., (eds.). *Faulkner, Modernism, and Film*, University Press of Mississippi, 1979.

Hilliard, Robert L. *Writing for Television and Radio*, Hastings House, 1976.

Jacobs, Lewis. *The Emergence of Film Art*, Hopkinson and Blake, 1969.

―――. *The Rise of the American Film*, Teachers College, 1968.

Kawin, Bruce F., *Faulkner and Film*, F. Ungar, 1977.

Leonard, William T. *Theatre: Stage to Screen to Television,* Scarecrow Press, 1981.

Magill, Frank N. *Cinema—the novel into film,* Salem Press, 1980.

Mascelli, Joseph V. *The Five C's of Cinematography,* Cine-Grafic Publications, 1965.

Mast, Gerald, *A Short History of the Movies,* Bobbs-Merrill, 1977.

Millerson, Gerald. *The Technique of Television Production,* Hastings House, 1974.

Newcomb, Horace. (Editor) *Television: The Critical View,* Oxford Press, 1979.

————. *TV: The Most Popular Art,* Anchor Press, 1974.

Ramsaye, Terry. *A Million and One Nights,* Simon and Schuster, 1964.

Ravage, John W. *Television, the director's viewpoint,* Westview Press, 1978.

Seldes, Gilbert. *The Public Arts,* Simon & Schuster, 1956.

Siepmann, Charles A. *Radio, Television, and Society,* Oxford Press, 1950.

Solomon, Stanley J. *The Film Idea,* Harcourt Brace Jovanovich, 1972.

Vidal, Gore. *Visit to a Small Planet and other Television Plays,* Little, Brown and Co., 1956.

Zettl, Herbert. *Sight-Sound-Motion,* Wadsworth Publishing Co., 1973.

————. *Television Production Handbook,* 1976.